The Pregnancy Decision Handbook

for Women with Depression

70 important questions to consider The
Pregnancy
Decision
Handbook

for Women with
Depression

Stephanie S. Durruthy, M.D.

mind
support, LLC

Ellicott City, MD

The Pregnancy Decision Handbook for Women with Depression
by Stephanie S. Durruthy, M.D.

Published 2005 by Mindsupport, LLC
Contact author in care of: Mindsupport, LLC, 5074 Dorsey Hall Dr., Ellicott City, MD 21042. Visit www.mindsupport.com or e-mail info@mindsupport.com.

DISCLAIMER: The author and publisher of this book have attempted to ensure that the information it contains is accurate and complete. Nonetheless, medicine and legislation are ever-changing. Therefore, the author and publisher of this book do not suggest that the information provided is in every way accurate and complete or will remain up to date, even in the near term. The author and publisher disclaim all responsibility for liability of use of this information for personal purposes. Readers should make their treatment decisions based upon the advice of their own physician. This book is to be used as a reference only and should not replace or be considered a substitute for the advice rendered by your health provider. You should discuss any conflicts with your own physician and should rely on the advice of your own physician.

Cover and interior design by Pneuma Books, LLC
For more info, visit www.pneumabooks.com
Printed in the United States of America by United Graphics, Inc.

Publisher's Cataloging-In-Publication
(Prepared by The Donohue Group)

Durruthy, Stephanie S.
    The pregnancy decision handbook for women with depression : 70 important questions to consider / Stephanie S. Durruthy.

    p. ; cm.
    Includes bibliographical references and index.
    ISBN-13: 978-0-9765814-1-3
    ISBN-10: 0-9765814-1-8

1. Pregnancy—Decision making—Popular works. 2. Pregnancy in mentally ill women—Popular works. 3. Human reproduction—Moral and ethical aspects—Popular works. I. Title.

RG526 .D87 2005
618.2/0874
10 9 08 07 06 05

LCCN: 2005922244
            6 5 4 3 2 1

To all the women who have guided me
in my life's journey

Contents

Foreword

The Pregnancy Decision Handbook is exactly that, a hands-on book, to be read, referred to, read again and again. Like a toolbox, it is there when you need it with the right tool — the right answer to the right question. It advocates that the patient be an informed consumer. Further it is a stinging reminder that it is incumbent upon all health care providers in clinical practice to provide information appropriately individualized to each patient regarding all possible outcomes of specified treatments.

This is a user friendly, tell what I need to know book. Reading it is like being in the office face to face with Dr. Durruthy. It conveys authenticity, the feeling of a personally likeable, trustworthy, competent, and life-experienced person. The book portrays the role of a psychiatrist at its best. It address the *whole person* and describes effectively how the *brain*, as one of the body's most powerful organs, must be understood in the interactive content of a specific individual in a specific environment. She repeats the basic caveat, pregnancy is not a disorder, depression is. She clarifies again and again common myths, fears, ignorance, and beliefs that may cause harm to pregnant women who are depressed or are vulnerable to depression.

The appeal of the book is the universality of both pregnancy and depression. Depression is one of the earliest and most common disorders known to mankind, be it described as melancholy, grief, sadness, despair. Pregnancy is life itself and female only (by definition), is capable of giving birth. Do not be misled by the easy flowing, no nonsense practical here and now approach. This book is an evidence-based work of a scientific scholar of principle and ethics. Her life-driven purpose has been to embody in daily practice the wholeness of women as a biologic, psychologic, socio-cultural entity. Attention must be paid in word and deed.

This book should be in every health care provider's office. It should be in public governmental offices and school libraries and would find welcome any place women in need and caregivers cross paths. Last, but not least, this handbook is of value for the references and resources alone. Kudos to Dr. Durruthy. I look forward to further editions.

— Julie Mayo, Ph.D., Clinical Professor of Psychiatry, Emeritus, New York Medical College

Preface

My name is Stephanie Durruthy. I am a female, a wife, a mommy, and a psychiatrist. These demographics might be important for those of you considering pregnancy, since I have been there, done that... As a mom with a daughter in elementary school, I can still vividly recall the trials and joys of being pregnant. As a psychiatrist in clinical practice, I have explored childbearing issues with numerous patients in view of their illness.

This project was developed as a tool to address the complex topic of depression and pregnancy. Unfortunately, many women with mood disorders base their decision about childbearing on myths. These myths include concepts about mild antidepressants, fetal exposure to medications preventing future illness, and depressive illness contraindicating pregnancy.

This book was written to be thought-provoking and empowering. It was created as an educational tool for women with clinical depression as they address the complex issues of pregnancy with their health provider. The intent of the project is to be used as an information resource for informed decision making. Although this book is intended to be used as a reference, it is not intended as medical advice for the reader and should not be used as a substitute or replacement for the advice rendered by your health provider. If anything in this text conflicts with the advice rendered by your health provider, you should discuss this with your health care provider and should rely on his or her advice.

Acknowledgments

I would like to thank: Abby Durruthy, my physician-father who taught me the essence of medicine is the patient relationship. Kristen, my daughter who increased my listening sensitivity for mommy concerns. Diane E. Stabler, MD, board-certified child and adult psychiatrist, who spent countless hours supporting me with this project. Carol A. McKenzie, MD, board certified obstetrician and gynecologist, whose clinical insights were a priceless asset. Delores P. Byrd, Employee Relations Manager for the DC Public Schools, whose extensive knowledge of employee benefits was a wonderful resource. Lynn Clements, for her creative editorial abilities. Beverly Berry, who organized my clinical practice, for me to make time for this book. My patients, who challenge me to maintain my knowledge of the latest treatment options. My husband, loving family, friends and mentors who nurture and sustain me. My Creator for bestowing upon me my many blessings.

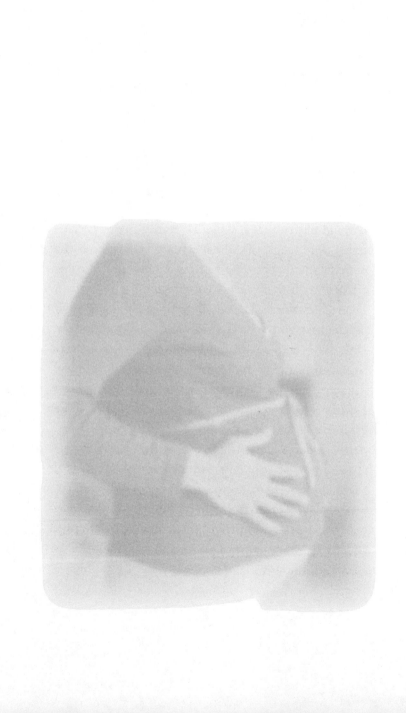

Introduction

During my twenty years of clinical practice, a topic often explored is the issue of pregnancy for women with depressive illness. My response to these inquiries of pregnancy and parenting has changed over the years. There has been a dramatic increase in clinical information about pregnancy and depression. Personally, the birth of my daughter nine years ago changed the way I counsel patients about pregnancy issues. No longer was the pregnancy-planning discussion just an analysis of patient symptoms of illness, treatment alternatives, and a risk versus benefit documentation of treatment options.

My pregnancy was joyful and uneventful, and this

personal life experience sensitized me to the difficulties females may encounter with both pregnancy and parenting. My listening ear is now fine-tuned to hear and understand the irrational worries of pregnancy. I am excited to share in the midst of these complex conversations about pregnancy the clinical advances in the field of psychiatric reproductive health. My clinical experience allows me to affirm that women who are empowered with knowledge about their illness, have a support system, and plan their pregnancies have better outcomes.

As patient treatment options become more and more complicated, I believe there is a need for patient resources that are easy to understand. I am a firm believer in patient education. In my office, I have plenty of resources available for patient information. When I give lectures, I always leave the audience with handouts for information. Yet, I could not find a resource for my patients with depression to address their concerns about pregnancy decision-making. I found myself interpreting physician information given to me by the pharmaceutical companies and reviewing scientific studies when they really needed a resource they could easily read and come back to again and again.

This book fills this void in patient information on this topic. I really enjoy teaching, and this became an educational tool. I wanted to create a thought-provoking handbook that triggered further questions, would easily supplement other information, clear up misinformation, but not dictate clinical decision-making.

My goal is for this handbook to be user-friendly, interactive, and an easy read, even for those with attention difficulties. It seemed ideal under the guidance of my editors, Pneuma Books, that the final book product would be in a question-answer format.

I have realized over the years that my patients' concerns and questions about childbearing with depressive illness are universal. Even question and answer sessions in community forums contain the same frequently asked questions about pregnancy and depression.

Gradually my lecture notes and years of clinical expertise on this topic grew to fill this handbook.

My patients routinely bring me medical information they have obtained from newspapers, articles in the popular press, the Internet, and health commentaries. Many times the information is contradictory. I use the information brought to me as a launching for developing their individualized treatment plan. Medical information must be tailored to the individual patient's treatment plan by their own health professional, who understands both their medical history and their risk factors.

May this handbook be a resource for your "maybe baby" decision.

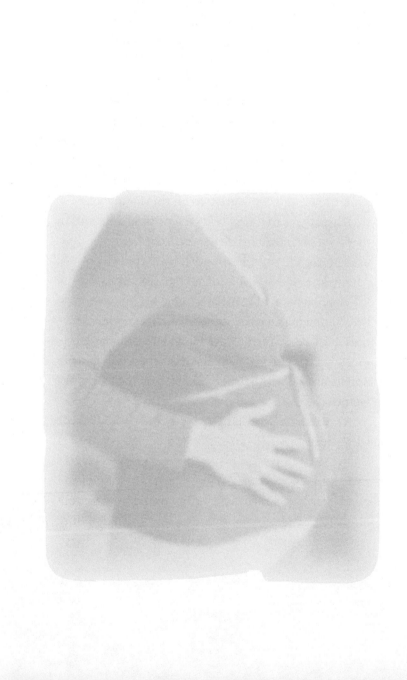

Chapter 1

Is the Pregnancy Journey for Me?

Parenting is a gift and challenge. There comes a time in every woman's life when she addresses her childbearing potential. The baby question could lead to a decision for sterilization, use of contraceptives to prevent pregnancy, or an intense preoccupation with her biological clock and procreation.

When a female with depressive illness considers pregnancy, the symptoms of that illness can complicate childbearing issues. The patient with depressive illness has to acknowledge her symptoms of depression and then plan how she will deal with them during her pregnancy. Pregnancy will not cure depressive illness.

1. What are some of the pregnancy requirements for a healthy baby?

It takes approximately nine months for a baby to develop in a woman's body. The baby's best chance to be healthy is for its mother to take care of herself. Pregnancy planning gives the mother-to-be an opportunity to make those healthy behavior changes that she may have postponed.

Women with depressive illness have a higher incidence of cigarette smoking, increased alcohol consumption, substance abuse, and poor nutritional choices. Planning a pregnancy could give the future mommy the opportunity to make healthy behavioral changes for herself that will increase her potential for a healthy child.

The best baby outcome requires prenatal care. The to do list will add additional tests and regular obstetrical visits to your usual schedule of mental health appointments. Many women with active depressive symptoms feel overwhelmed with daily living, let alone additional scheduled activities. Some physicians do not work on weekends or evenings, which will require additional planning.

Underlying physical illness will also need to be addressed. If you have a medical illness, the pregnancy will require it be under control or monitored carefully during prenatal care. I have met many females with depressive illness who neglect diseases such as asthma and hypertension. If you have neglected such health issues, you'll need time to get those illnesses stabilized before you get pregnant. Your untreated medical problem could only get worst with pregnancy and impact you and your baby. Pregnancy does not cure disease.

2. **What can be the initial signs of pregnancy?**
   - Missed menstrual period
   - Fatigue
   - Nausea with and without vomiting
   - Breast tenderness and tingling of the breast
   - Metallic taste in the mouth
   - Frequent urination [1]

3. **What can I expect with pregnancy?**
   Every woman's experience with pregnancy is unique. Many, many books have been published to satisfy the need to accurately predict the pregnancy experience. I can accurately predict that you will not have a menstrual period for at least nine months while pregnant, your belly should grow, and you should gain some weight.

   What follows are events that may occur in each trimester of pregnancy. You may have all or none of these symptoms.

   First Trimester (1 – 13 weeks)

   Physical Possibilities
   - Extreme fatigue due to reproductive hormones
   - Nausea and vomiting common in half of pregnancies
   - Metallic taste in your mouth

- Increased urination due to bladder compression by an enlarging uterus
- Breast tenderness and tingling by the first month
- Increase in breast size with tiny veins visible beneath the skin by the second month
- An increase in whitish, vaginal secretions called leukorrhea
- Headaches
- Increased appetite but generally little weight gains (1.5 to 3 lbs.)

Emotional Possibilities
- Mood swings similar to your premenstrual experience — irritability, laughing, and unprovoked crying all within a few hours
- Worries about the pregnancy, especially if it is an "oops" baby
- Concerns about fetal exposure if medications were present
- Ambivalence about the pregnancy
- Concerns about the chosen depression treatment if abrupt changes have been implemented because of the pregnancy
- Depressive illness may improve or relapse

Second Trimester (14 – 27 weeks)

Physical Possibilities
- Fatigue

- Constipation due to slower intestinal movements, pregnancy hormones, and iron supplements
- Increased urinary frequency with awakening to pass urine four times a night being normal
- Nausea and vomiting of morning sickness significantly reduced
- Increased vaginal secretions
- Increased body weight reflects maternal growth of the placenta, uterus, and blood volume
- Clothes fit snugly
- Dizziness
- Gum bleeding
- Headaches reduced
- Breast enlargement
- Mild swelling of ankles and feet
- Irregular, painless uterine contractions (Braxton Hicks) at twenty weeks
- Insomnia due to nighttime urination
- Baby movements
- Backache
- Irregular brown patches on face and neck (chloasma or the mask of pregnancy)
- Hemorrhoids
- Heartburn (reflux esophagitis)

Emotional Possibilities
- Increased mood swings of irritability, down spells, and crying spells similar to premenstrual period

- Improved emotional stability or worsening of depressive illness
- Foggy thinking, concentration, and memory impairment

Third Trimester (28 – 40 weeks or delivery)

Physical Possibilities
- Baby weight gain — generally about one pound per week with the average total healthy weight gain for a woman being twenty-five – thirty pounds
- Increased heartburn due to the growing baby
- Sensation of increased pressure in the pelvic area
- Perception of tingling or numbness in the upper extremities.
- Increased generalized swelling of hands, feet, and eyes with a fifty percent increase in blood and fluid
- Increased insomnia due to baby movements and frequent urination
- Increased back pain
- Decreased walking stance
- Constipation
- Increased urinary frequency
- Rhythmic uterine contractions that may occur every ten to twenty minutes, causing discomfort or false labor
- Severe leg cramps

Emotional Possibilities
- Increased mood swings, irritability, and crying spells

- Worries and fears increase about the labor and delivery process
- Increased concerns about a healthy baby
- Increased anxiety about getting to the hospital on time for delivery
- Increased worries about childcare if planning to work
- Increased concerns about postpartum depression
- Depressive illness can increase or improve
- Continued foggy thinking and impaired concentration

4. **Why did you group the pregnancy journey into trimesters?**

I am a psychiatrist who often has to treat women with medications. During pregnancy planning discussions, minimizing fetal exposure during the initial thirteen weeks of organ development while maintaining remission of patient symptoms becomes the initial treatment plan. If the pregnancy can be planned, I try to identify the safest and most effective agent for fetal exposure to medication during these critical first weeks. Not every woman with depressive illness requires medications with their pregnancy, but some do.

Ideally, the treatment that has kept a woman symptom-free before pregnancy should be continued. However, some of my patients, despite their risk of relapse, want to discontinue medication or significantly reduce their medication dose during pregnancy. These changes in their treatment plan will require even closer monitoring for depression relapse. Each trimester becomes very important, as we negotiate for treatment options based upon the presence or absence of symptoms.

If the patient's symptoms have increased during the second trimester, medication increases or reintroduction of medications may be required. The final trimester requires close monitoring for relapse of illness, increased risk factors of adverse outcomes, and a possible episode of postpartum disorder.

5. **Should I consider the impact of my depressive illness on my parenting responsibilities and my expectations for baby development?**

Many books have been published to satisfy the demand for knowledge about parenting babies. One can easily obtain books about potential parental responsibilities for babies on a week-to-week or a month-to-month basis. As a person with depressive illness reads these reference materials about baby development and parental expectations, they should consider their active illness and how it may impact their ability to provide care. A successful pregnancy with the birth of a healthy baby does not eliminate the impact of underlying depressive illness.

Many women with depressive illness describe parenting as rewarding and fulfilling. Others acknowledge the positive aspects of being a parent but caution that it can be emotionally and physically draining. As a woman with depressive illness considers the demands of caring for a newborn, which can be draining for someone without depression, her illness can become a key factor in determining her ability to successfully parent. If her depressive symptoms are not in total remission, it can limit her ability to take on new challenges.

6. **What should a person with depressive illness consider when they read books about baby development and parenting expectations?**

Symptoms of depressive illness can affect an individual's ability to provide consistent care for themselves and others. Think about these issues when considering pregnancy.

Sleep Deprivation

Can you function without sleep? There are individuals who require a minimal amount of restorative sleep hours and cannot function without it. Having a baby will not change what your brain requires for you to function at your best. Sleep deprivation can trigger depressive illness in vulnerable individuals. Many of my patients initially resist the suggestion to allow others to care for their newborn at night so they may sleep. Often only in response to worsening illness, sleep habits get restored. Restoring nighttime sleep can help many struggling new moms stabilize their moods.

Energy

Individuals with depressive illness often struggle with low energy stores. Being a new mom does not improve your baseline low energy state. Ideally, the mom with active depressive illness should assess daily how much energy is available in her reserve. Based upon this honest energy assessment, she can now determine what task, if any, can be completed. New moms often have no energy with a new baby. This lack of energy is only magnified when you add depressive illness to the situation.

Negativity

One's perception of life can immediately become negative, hopeless, and riddled with despair when a person with active depressive illness is confronted with unexpected change and transitions. A new baby means change. It is part of the baby's contract to require the parents to make permanent and unpredictable changes in their lifestyle.

Neutrality becomes important as it allows an individual with active depressive illness to experience life without the expectation of a negative outcome. Ideally, parents instill in their children positive encouragement and hope that they will achieve a better tomorrow. Active depressive illness does not excuse you from encouraging and providing positive outlooks for your child.

Nervousness

Active depressive symptoms can be associated with fears and anxieties about everyday life. A new baby is associated with unpredictable life events that can greatly increase the anxiety level of a person with depressive illness. These worries and fears have to be under control, or the child may be taught that the world is a scary place. Babies observe their caregivers. Assume a child watches their mother jump and scream every time the doorbell rings. Eventually a baby could mimic this behavior as a learned response to their environment.

Patience

A new baby can give a parent many opportunities to become frustrated. Newborns can continuously cry for no apparent reason. An inconsolable baby can be very difficult for any parent, but an individual with active depressive illness can potentially have extreme emotional reactions to normal care-giving frustrations. Impulsively shaking a crying baby to quiet him or her can cause a medical emergency. Symptoms of irritability and rage in a person with active depression can possibly trigger extreme impulsive emotional responses. Uncontrolled irritability and rage will not benefit any parent-child relationship.

Organization

Life is too overwhelming when depressive symptoms are active. The tasks of daily living can be impossible when a person is depressed. Basic activities such as getting out of bed in the morning, taking a bath, and making oneself a meal for breakfast can be extremely difficult with active depressive illness.

Parenting requires a person to take care of themselves and their baby. Babies function the best when they have a predictable schedule for their daily activities of feeding, naps, and stimulating activities. A routine makes a baby feel secure. Even when the caregiver is depressed and cannot function, the baby's schedule should not change. Secure babies require constant attention.

Socialization

Active depressive symptoms can make a person self-occupied with their despair, hopelessness, and negative thoughts. This depressive self-preoccupation is often magnified by low energy and being short fused. In this depressed emotional state, it is quite common that one's ability to tolerate the presence of others is limited.

Babies require socialization and stimulation to promote their verbal, social, and intellectual development. Active depressive illness can potentially inhibit the mother's ability to provide the stimulation required for the baby's development. Caring for a baby requires much more than insuring that they are fed and their diapers are changed. A baby is totally dependent upon the parent for care and nurturing.

Consistency

A baby feels secure when their needs are met. Your response to the baby should remain the same no matter how depressed you might feel. If your symptoms of depression are severe, you may be limited in your ability to consistently respond to your child. Extreme fatigue and poor concentration, often experienced with active illness, can become a barrier to childcare.

Frequent hospitalizations for stabilization of illness and depressive symptoms that are still active despite treatment can limit your availability for your child. Some treatments cause side effects that make you feel numb or sedated. Your baby will not understand your unavailability due to depressive illness. All babies just want their needs met by their caregivers.

Your Own Childhood Memories

I am a psychiatrist who treats adults. Despite my patients being over the age of twenty-one, some still vividly recall painful childhood memories regarding their mother's active symptoms of depression. Some feel that their early childhood experiences still impact negatively upon them. I have written the following snapshot memories with fictionalized names and stories. Nonetheless, the behaviors described are classic symptoms of depression.

My mother was never available. Most of the time, she spent in her bedroom with the door closed. My siblings and I raised each other. Being the oldest, I took care of my younger sisters and brothers. I never had a true childhood. Maybe that is why I never wanted any kids of my own.

— Tina, age 54

Our house was a mess. My mom was a full-time housewife but it was total chaos. There were clothes and garbage everywhere in the house. My three siblings and

I never bought any of our friends over. It was too embarrassing for anyone to see. My mom was just overwhelmed with raising us kids and chores. She cried constantly and promised daily to do better. It never happened.

— Karen, age 37

My mom was just mean. You never knew what to expect from her. One day a behavior was fine, while the next day the very same behavior would send her into a rage attack. She would scream, yell at us kids, and throw objects at us. One day, she shook me so hard, I thought my brain would pop out of my head. I am sure my dysfunctional childhood plays a role in my current anxiety.

— Louise, age 21

I used to see other moms play with their kids from my window. My mom never had time for me. She was always so tired and fatigued. The thought of just playing games and dolls was just too much. Mom was not sick, but she never had energy to do anything. I missed that mother-daughter special time.

— Diane, age 27

There was just drama in my house. My parents were always fighting. They would curse and scream at each other all the time. I was ten when I found my mother overdosed on pills after one of their fighting matches. I went into her bedroom to kiss her good night only to find her unconscious on the floor with pills scattered all around her. I called 911.

— *Tina, age 34*

My mom was so negative. She never had a positive word of encouragement. No matter how much I tried to get her approval and support, it was never given. Mom always felt the world was a hopeless place and then you die. Now as an adult I see myself like my mother with her pessimism and hopelessness.

— *Maria, age 41*

My mother did not believe in the benefits of playmates and socializing. We lived in a dark house with the blinds closed until Dad came home from work in the evening. She believed that people just wanted to harm you and that the neighborhood kids were all troublemakers. Mom had no friends. History does repeat itself in my case. I feel very uncomfortable in any social setting. Overall I consider myself a loner.

— *Kristen, age 30*

The decision to have a child is not just about you. Kids require attention 24/7. If you have depressive illness, can you stabilize your illness? If not, do you have a support system that can help you raise your child?

Now that you are aware of the issues associated with pregnancy, let us consider the impact of clinical depression on the situation.

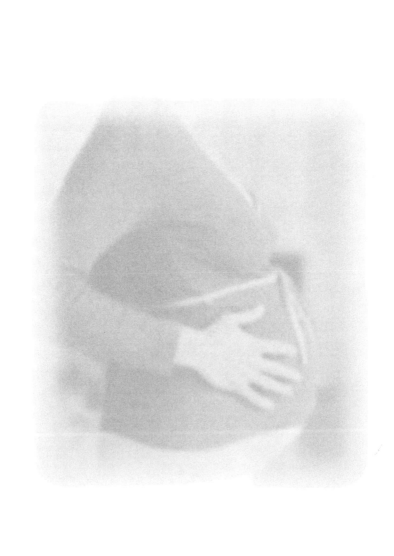

Chapter 2

Is This Depressive Illness or Just a Bad Hair Day?

The human brain gets no respect, it seems. The onset of unexplained chest pain, a fever, and evidence of blood in the urine can trigger an immediate emergency room visit. Abnormal bodily functions prompt most individuals to quickly find an answer to their problems. Meanwhile, many individuals who can readily recognize new or abnormal mood reactions wait for months before addressing their condition. The decision to ignore problematic emotional reactions and behaviors is very common.

Mood symptoms that suggest underlying brain problems are initially subtle but progress in frequency and intensity until finally a crisis develops. Depressive symptoms such as insomnia, decreased appetite, unprovoked crying spells, and poor concentration are familiar to the human experience, which can prevent the recognition of illness. Situational stressors, such as marital problems, can be seen as the cause of emotional problems rather than the onset of depressive illness being the cause of the emotional problems.

The difficulties with the recognition and acceptance of depressive illness can be magnified by the fears associated with the stigma of mental illness, memories of emotionally impaired family members, cultural values, and the perception that depressive illness is a weakness. I have told many patients to refer to me not as their psychiatrist, but as the cardiologist of their brain if this allows them to accept the diagnosis more easily.

7. Are sadness and clinical depression the same problem?

In retrospect, Sigmund Freud and the other founders of psychiatry should have named clinical "depression" something else. People get so confused about the differences between a depression you treat with pills and the feelings of sadness, which you can control. A bout of moderate to severe clinical depression rarely can be relieved by will power alone. You cannot vacation, shop till you drop, or fine dine to make an episode of severe clinical depression disappear. No matter what you do to rid yourself of significant symptoms, it persists despite your best effort to make it disappear. By the time most patients decide to seek professional help, they have become powerless against their symptoms.

8. **Is it that important to be "labeled" with a mental illness diagnosis?**

Some patients tell me that they have spells of depression for which their primary care physician gives them some pills to alleviate the symptoms.

But there are different types of depression, all of which have different outcomes and prognoses. The correct diagnosis is the cornerstone for the best treatment. The consideration of treatment options for depression during pregnancy requires the correct diagnosis and determination of the severity of your illness.

9. **What are the symptoms of a clinical depression versus sadness?**

The American Psychiatric Association Diagnostic and Statistical Manual of Mental Disorders DSMIV suggests that the diagnosis of a Major Depressive Episode be given to the following symptoms. In order to meet the criteria, five or more of the following symptoms must be present during a two-week period.

- depressed mood most of the day
- diminished interests in activities or pleasurable activities
- significant weight loss, decrease or increase in appetite
- restlessness or slowness observed by others

- fatigue or loss of energy
- blaming oneself too much and feeling worthless
- inability to make decisions or concentrate
- insomnia or sleeping too much
- thinking about death frequently[2]

These symptoms must cause clinically significant distress in social, occupational, or self-functioning situations.

10. **What are the different types of depression?**

There are depressive symptoms that have an obvious trigger as the source of the mood. Often with removal of the stress, physical illness, toxin, or situation, the symptom of depression will disappear. The following would be considered in that category.

A Substance-Induced Mood Disorder

Cocaine and alcohol abuse can trigger bouts of depression.

Mood Disorder Due to a General Medical Condition

Symptoms of hypothyroidism can mimic a bout with clinical depression.

Bereavement

Immediate losses of loved ones can trigger depressive symptoms.

Adjustment Disorder with Depressed Mood

Situations such as job stress, marital discord, divorce, and financial issues can trigger a bout of depression. Generally, the mood improves once the situation is resolved.[3]

If you have these types of depression and are considering pregnancy, the treatment option should be easy. One should resolve or eliminate the trigger or situation in order to manage the depressive illness. Unfortunately, life can be complicated. Stressful situations cannot be so readily resolved and require other intervention.

The dilemma of treatment for depression and pregnancy becomes much more serious when the symptoms are caused by brain disease and the person has a family history of depression. The following would be considered in that category.

Major Depressive Episodes

These are generally characterized by a loss of interest or pleasure or a depressed mood for a minimum of two weeks. These symptoms are accompanied by significant impairment in social functioning, occupational functioning, and self-care.

Dysthymia

This is a chronic depression that waxes and wanes in intensity. If you have a lot of stress in your life, you feel your symptoms more intensely; if life is good, you can still feel your illness somewhat, but it's not so intense. This type of depression never goes away completely. If you do not feel the depression today, you can predict it will come back within two month's time.

Bipolar I Disorder

This is a depressive type that has similar symptoms to a major depressive illness, but it also has intervals of elated, irritable, or euphoric moods that can trigger dysfunctional behavior or dangerous impulsivity. These mood swings can be severe and require psychiatric hospitalization.

Bipolar II Disorder

This has similar symptoms to a major depressive illness in the context of intervals with elation, euphoria, or irritability that triggers dysfunctional behavior whose severity does not require hospitalization.

Schizoaffective Disorder

This is a type of depression that has the complexity of both symptoms of a major depressive illness and schizophrenia.[4]

11. **Are all the treatments for clinical depression the same regardless of the type?**

The type of depressive illness will determine the recommended treatment and outcome. Despite episodes of depression, bipolar illness often requires the use of mood stabilizing agents in addition to the use of antidepressant medications. This book will focus on treatment options for clinical depression without the consideration of other diagnostic possibilities.

12. **How do mental health professionals determine the difference between mild, moderate, and severe depression?**

Depression can cause significant distress or impairment in social and work function. Many persons who have the illness of depression would assume any symptom is severe. Yet, clinicians grade depressive illness severity based upon the number of symptoms reported and the person's level of functioning.

Mild Symptoms Category Requires Two Parts in Order to Qualify

First, you must have identified a few depressive symptoms. Second, you must be able to take care of your personal care needs, do well with your household chores, work well on the job, and interact socially with little or no impairment.

Moderate Symptoms Category Requires Two Parts in Order to Qualify

First, you must have identified several symptoms of depression. Second, you have some difficulty with self-care, household chores, job responsibilities, and social interaction.

Severe Symptoms Category Requires Two Parts in Order to Qualify

First, you must have endorsed almost all of the symptoms of depression. Second, that you have significant difficulty in your usual daily functions — work, social, and self-care. An example would be a patient who cannot go to work or is unable to care for herself or take care of her children.[5]

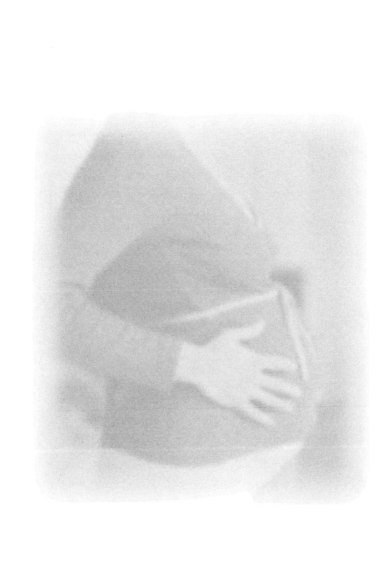

Chapter 3

Identifying My Risk Factors for Depressive Illness

Depression is often described as a chemical imbalance. It is a disease state similar to those of other body organs such as the pancreas and thyroid. Illness occurs in the brain when the mood hormones or chemicals are not at the levels required to sustain a normal mood.

13. Can depression be inherited?

Often a person with depressive illness has a family member with symptoms similar to their own. The incidence of depression can be increased with a family history, or as I tell my patients, the passage of the family jewels can occur throughout the generations. Yet extensive family history does not guarantee a person will have the illness. Despite the ongoing excitement with the twenty-year-old National Institute of Mental Health (NIMH) Human Genetics Initiative project, the medical community still does not have the tools to accurately predict depressive illness based upon genetics.[6]

14. My mother has a history of recurrent depression, and I have a history of moderate depression. What does that mean for a baby?

Your baby would have a higher risk of having difficulty with depression. A positive family history increases the risk but does not guarantee illness. A new area of research is exploring the risk of illness inheritance based upon the number of family members with chronic versus episodic bouts of illness. It appears that families with histories of chronic illness might have a higher risk of inheritance than those with family members who report a brief bout of depression. [7]

Oftentimes there are numerous family members with undiagnosed depressive illness. Many cultures cannot accept mental illness because of fears and ignorance about treatment. Persons with depressive illness often identify family members with symptoms similar to themselves by historical details. Alcoholism, suicide, and psychiatric hospitalization are often family secrets never discussed, which hinders the assessment of a patient's risk factors.

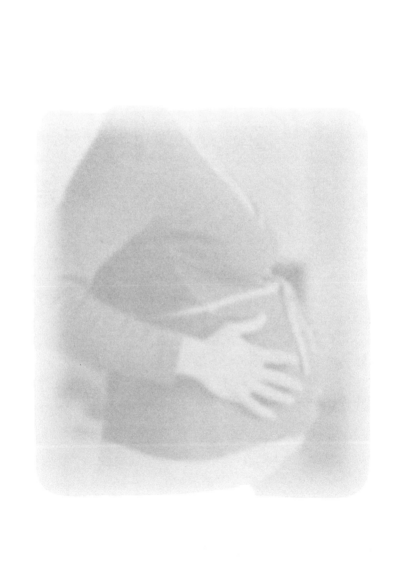

Chapter 4

Depression, Pregnancy, and Me

The risk for an onset of depression increases among childbearing women.[8] It is a myth that pregnancy will prevent the onset of depressive illness. Between ten and sixteen percent (10% – 16%) of women experience clinically significant depression during pregnancy.[9]

15. **What are the identified risk factors for women during pregnancy?**

- A prior history of depression
- Marital discord or dissatisfaction
- Limited social support
- Recent adverse life events
- Family history of depression

- Lower socioeconomic status[10]
- Unwanted pregnancy
- Young age of motherhood[11]

16. Are there physical signs that someone will see that suggest I am depressed?

When someone has responded to treatment for depression, there are no physical signs to suggest it. Yet, when someone's depressive illness is active, their behaviors are easily identifiable. The symptoms of crying for no reason, forgetfulness, and marked irritability are some symptoms that can occur when a person is having difficulty with depression. These behaviors will often identify the person as having some problem.

17. Can I function daily with my symptoms of depression?

In order to consider treatment options, you will first have to assess the impact that depression has upon you. In your daily world, can you function when you feel your illness? Some individuals become so self-absorbed with their emotions that they lose touch with reality. A person can feel very misunderstood, overwhelmed with their marriage, and total hopelessness because of their depression. Once in treatment, they realize they felt overwhelmed because of the depression, not their circumstances. It would have been a mistake to have divorced their spouse or quit their job. Yet, the immediate feelings of depression are so intense that it is very hard to recognize these as irrational mood signals.

18. What about my duties and responsibilities?

Everyone has daily duties and responsibilities. You may be just responsible for yourself. Others might have to support both their immediate and extended families. Some women have partners who are present but not emotionally supportive or involved in household affairs. A weekly paycheck can be required for survival for some. If so, being bedridden with a complication of pregnancy and depressive illness would be catastrophic. The course of pregnancy and outcome is unpredictable. Proper planning for all the possibilities allows you to think through your choices and plan, so life can be less stressful during pregnancy.

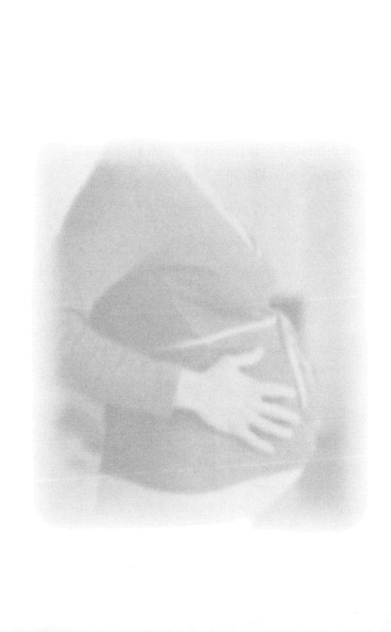

Chapter 5

Baby, Money, and Me

Uneventful pregnancy is considered a normal life event and is not considered a covered benefit by most disability insurance companies.

19. Will I be able to support myself if I'm pregnant and become depressed while employed?

If you become severely depressed, your symptoms may interfere with your work function. If a mental health professional can attribute this interference to your illness, you may qualify for disability compensation. Start to ask your employer's human resources manager for the details of your company's benefit terms. Inquire about your disability policy with regards to its elimination period and benefit terms. The elimination period is the required number of days without payment from your first day off work until you become eligible for disability money. Under the 1978 Pregnancy Discrimination Act, a problem pregnancy must be treated like any other disability.[12]

20. I always feel my symptoms of depression. Could I just file for long-term disability during my pregnancy for financial support?

The goal of treatment is to enable you to return to work as soon as possible. Disability support is typically for a brief period while you get the symptoms that interfere with your work function under control. The goal of your disability policy is not to support you financially until you become symptom free. Your mental health provider would have to document your continued lack of response to treatment in order to qualify for continuation of payment. Psychiatry offers so many treatment options that it is unlikely that you would remain impaired. Long-term disability assumes that you will not return to work at your former employer because of your illness. If you are not employed, you will lose your health benefits. Even the COBRA extension of health benefits if you are unemployed may not be a viable alternative because one must pay the entire medical premium during the eighteen-month extension period.

21. **Will the Family and Medical Leave Act of 1993 (FMLA) protect my job if I have a relapse of my depression while pregnant and require long-term leave?**

The Family and Medical Leave Act of 1993 is a federal law that would provide employees the opportunity to take up to twelve weeks of non-paid leave during any twelve-month period for the following events.

- The birth and subsequent care of a newborn child of an employee
- The placement of a child through either adoption or foster care with an employee
- The care of an immediate family member with a serious health problem
- A medical leave when the employee themselves is unable to work due to their own serious health condition

Under FMLA the employer must hold your job for you, or offer an equivalent one, if you return to work within the twelve-month period. Not all companies are required to obey the Family and Medical Leave Act of 1993. The number of employees in the company is an important factor to determine legal participation. FMLA generally applies to all companies who have at least fifty or more employees within a seventy - five-mile radius of the work location. If you work for a small business, you probably do not have the same legal protections as a large Fortune 500 company would provide. It is best to do personal research about your company and then

ask your human resource person or your boss about their
maternity leave policy.[13]

22. My frequent bouts of severe depression will probably require the use of FMLA during my pregnancy, but I cannot afford to have weeks without pay. What can I do?

Pregnancies that are planned afford the greatest potential for mood stabilization. While planning your pregnancy, you may consider accumulating your leave and vacation days for your anticipated maternity leave. Some companies have a family leave bank to borrow from other employees, while other businesses allow employee compensatory time for overtime hours, which can be accumulated in anticipation of illness. Money considerations require planning, especially when pregnancy and depression are being considered.

Financial worries can be a significant life stress, which can trigger a bout of depression in a person vulnerable for this illness. Further information can be obtained from these sources.

- Federal FMLA information can be obtained from your nearest office of Wage and Hour Division listed in the telephone directories under U.S. Government, Department of Labor, Employment Standards Administration or by dialing 866-487-9243. Their website is http://www.dol.gov/esa.

- Contact your individual State Labor Department for guidelines.

- For information about the Pregnancy Discrimination Act, you may contact EEOC. u.s. Equal Employment Opportunity Commission, 1801 L Street, N.W., Washington, D.C. 20507. You can contact them by phone at 202-663-4900 or be automatically connected to your nearest field office by calling 800-669-4000.

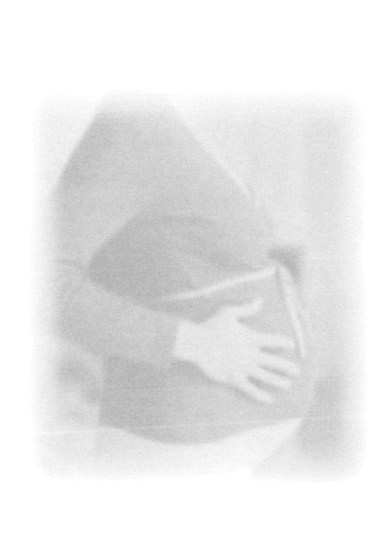

Chapter 6

Options
for
Treatment

Despite popular belief, pregnancy is not protective against depression. Being pregnant and/or having a baby does not prevent depressive illness. Current research does not support the myth that pregnancy is protective against depression.[14] In other words, if you have a history of prior depression or risk factors for illness, pregnancy will not prevent it. Let's address some options in your illness management.

23. What are the treatment options for depression in a pregnant woman?

There are various treatment recommendations for depression. Some females opt for no treatment, while others choose one or a combination of treatment options such as psychotherapy, light therapy, ECT, and medication.

If you are already in treatment, often the rule of thumb is to keep on doing whatever is keeping you emotionally well. This recommendation assumes that you have had a detailed risk versus benefit analysis with your mental health provider. This statement also assumes that the current treatment has safety data concerning pregnancy that you can accept.

I understand that many women and their families are afraid of the stigma of seeking treatment for mental illness, while others feel that depression is a normal event during pregnancy and choose not to seek intervention. However, medical research has informed us from both animal and human studies that untreated depression can pose risks.

Several research studies now suggest that maternal depression can cause significant problems for the unborn child, which can affect its development.

The actual mechanism that could explain these observations remains unknown. It has been hypothesized that the mother's mental state during pregnancy may negatively influence a developing baby by two pathways. First, the biological effects of maternal depression can adversely effect the placenta and/or cause hormonal changes, which can affect the fetus.[15] Second, there may be increased risk of poor lifestyle choices because of untreated maternal depression. These choices may include substance abuse, alcohol consumption, smoking cigarettes, and poor nutritional status. All of these factors can increase the risk of poor outcome during pregnancy and can be associated with low birth weight for the infant and the probability of pre-term delivery.

If untreated depression progresses in the mother, it can develop into severe stages, which can increase the risk of suicide and homicide.

24. I have not chosen intervention with a particular treatment, should I have another action plan?

It is always important to have an action plan for a possible relapse of depression. Having to explore options when in crisis often limits your options for treatment.

25. Are there non-medication treatments for depression?

The cornerstone of treatment for clinical depression has been psychotherapy. Psychoanalysis, a form of psychotherapy, and institutionalization were the only treatment options available for mental illness until the discovery of medication treatments in the mid 1900s. Better tools for diagnosis and public service announcements have increased the recognition of emotional illness. Mental illness has become the second frequent cause of activity limitation in adults from ages 18 – 44 in the United States.[16]

The decision to pursue treatment for a bodily ailment is often determined by the severity of the symptoms and how it inhibits personal functioning. Over the years, numerous treatment options have evolved. Often the decision to select a particular treatment option is determined by whether the symptoms are mild, moderate, or severe. Emotional symptoms that are becoming progressively worse and are inhibiting personal lifestyle will often prompt health-seeking behaviors with traditional mental health professionals.

Mild clinical depression is characterized by a few recognizable symptoms that have minimal or no impact on daily functioning. Many individuals with mild symptoms have sought relief with over the counter nutritional supplements such as St John's Wort. Others have pursued alternative treatments such as acupuncture, yoga, and Reiki. There are numerous treatment options advertised in the popular health marketplaces for mild depressive symptoms that do not interfere with one's ability to function.

Psychotherapy or "talk treatment" is foundational for non-medication stabilization of all severities of depressive symptoms. There are various types of talk treatment available, some with demonstrated research outcome and others with a legacy of good prognosis. Other novel treatments options such as light therapy and repetitive trans-cranial magnetic stimulation are being reviewed for possible consideration to stabilize depression during pregnancy. Electroshock therapy (ECT) has been available to pregnant women for decades as a non-medication option for severe depression.

26. What is psychotherapy?

Stedman's Medical Dictionary defines psychotherapy as the "treatment of emotional, behavioral, personality, and psychiatric disorders based primarily upon verbal or nonverbal communication and interventions with the patient…"[17]

27. Is psychotherapy an effective form of treatment for depression?

Psychotherapy, also known as talk therapy, can be an effective form of treatment for most types of depression. The exception being severe bouts of depressive illness, which may not respond to psychotherapy alone.

28. What are the most effective types of psychotherapy for maternal depression?

For years, researchers have been trying to develop scientific protocols to assess the most effective forms of psychotherapy. Not all types of psychotherapy can be easily translated into formats of manuals or scripts required for scientific research. Most mental health providers would agree that it is very difficult to quantify all "talking relationships" that can provide clinical benefit. However, interpersonal psychotherapy (ITP) is a type of therapy that has demonstrated positive outcomes during pregnancy in research studies.[18]

In the 1980s, Klerman and Weissman developed interpersonal psychotherapy (ITP). The therapist closely follows a manual or script to guide the patient in this highly structured treatment. It is time limited and the manual dictates what the client can bring to session for discussion. The focus of ITP is to resolve the numerous interpersonal relationship conflicts that can stem from the pregnancy and childbirth. This form of treatment has been readily adapted into formats for research study.[19]

Cognitive behavioral therapy is the other type of psychotherapy referred to for its positive research results during pregnancy. The basis of treatment is to correct the negative and maladaptive thinking process that a person with depressive illness experiences in life events. This form of psychotherapy assumes that if an individual is able to identify and correct distorted thinking processes, it will allow the patient to improve mood and establish both healthy emotional attitudes and coping mechanisms with stressful life events.[20]

Other popular therapies used during pregnancy by therapists that do not have scientific studies for outcome are both psychodynamic and supportive psychotherapies. The fundamental theory of psychodynamic therapy assumes that the basis of depressive symptoms is not in the conscious awareness of the individual with depressive illness. During treatment, the therapist assists the patient to uncover and correct these internal conflicts, which are often rooted in their childhood experiences.

In supportive psychotherapy, the therapist's focus is to solve the client's presenting complaint. The therapist offers guidance and suggestions for the patient's problems and issues. This non-structured, non-directed treatment does not always follow research protocols, which allows easy assessment in scientific outcome testing. Nonetheless, these non-structured therapies can provide benefit to certain individuals by stabilizing depressive symptoms during pregnancy.

Overall, psychotherapy can be a very effective form of treatment for depression during pregnancy. It is often recommended alone or in combination with medication.[21]

29. What does psychotherapy mean for me and my depression during pregnancy if I have situations that can often trigger a depressed mood?

Psychotherapy can be a very effective form of treatment. Many have found it useful in developing new coping skills for life's unpredictable, stressful moments. Others have found psychotherapy useful in resolving stressful relationships that trigger their depression. Psychotherapy has helped many resolve their poor self-esteem issues. Overall, psychotherapy remains a useful treatment to many individuals.

30. How can a therapist help me?

Once the triggers for your depressed mood have been identified, a therapist can help you resolve that issue into emotional peace. A therapist can help guide you to identify coping mechanisms and solutions for your depressive upheavals. Mild to moderate depression during pregnancy might respond to increased frequency of psychotherapy visits. You might consider seeing your therapist every two weeks, every week, or even twice a week during crisis. It is important to identify your triggers of illness and coping mechanisms for them.

31. Do I really need a therapist or a good self-help book?

Emotional issues that trigger significant emotional pain often require professional guidance. In order to resolve a painful issue, you would need to revisit the event emotionally, look at it, mourn it, and eventually discard it. A person reading a book by himself or herself will not relive and fully experience a painful emotional event. The brain has too many protective mechanisms to limit pain by forgetting or permitting selective recall.

32. How can I find a good therapist?

One important factor to determine successful therapy outcome is your comfort vibes with the therapist. If you trust and feel comfortable with your therapist, you will be able to share honestly your innermost feelings, which is necessary for ultimate emotional peace. Here are some other options for finding a therapist.

- Word of mouth or friends
- Referral — associations, social worker, psychologist, psychiatrist, licensed professional counselor
- Insurance networks if you are limited financially by the restraints of your insurance
- Specialty associations — depression-related disorders associations, anxiety disorders associations, NAMI, eating disorders associations
- Your health providers — primary care physician, gynecologist
- Local hospital staff referral networks

33. **What factors might be important for me in the selection of a therapist?**

The selection of a suitable therapist requires you to be honest with yourself. Some people feel much more at ease with a gender-specific therapist. Others realize that their attendance would increase if the therapist's office were in close proximity to their job.

A referral to a provider with a good reputation can be much more important in the selection process than being on a provider network. Culture-specific and language requirements may make some more comfortable. But what is most important is to find a therapist that makes you feel comfortable and that you can trust.

34. **Could light therapy help me during my pregnancy?**

Light therapy is an effective form of treatment for individuals who experience the symptoms of depression triggered by sensitivity to the lack of light or change of season. Chronobiological treatment, or light therapy, requires exposure to a specialized electrical appliance with a minimum light intensity of 10,000 lux. Under the appropriate guidance of a qualified health professional, phototherapy can be an effective form of treatment for this type of depression.

A few studies have suggested that light therapy may be an effective form of treatment for depression that is not seasonal. Included in these pilot studies are data for the use of light therapy in pregnancy. Early findings from a small sample-size research study of pregnant women suggest that sixty minutes daily of light therapy, beginning within ten minutes of awakening in the morning, could potentially stabilize depressed mood. These research results would have to be duplicated in other larger studies before it could become a recommendation for depression in pregnancy.[22] To use a light box to treat non-seasonal mild to moderate depression during pregnancy is considered experimental and should be done only under the close supervision of your mental health professional.

35. When is electroshock therapy (ECT) recommended?

ECT is an effective form of treatment for severe depression. When ECT is used in pregnancy, reports of complications are uncommon. For over fifty years, electroshock therapy (ECT) has been used safely during pregnancy. This form of treatment will affect the mother's brain directly to induce a required seizure but not affect the baby. The uterus is formed of smooth muscle which does not routinely contract during the seizure induced by ECT. Case reports of uterine contraction after ECT are few in number and usually did not cause premature labor. Malnourishment and dehydration are potential risk factors, and they may explain some cases of adverse outcomes associated with ECT.[23]

Mothers who are severely depressed with acute suicidal or loss of reality symptoms have found ECT to be an important option in their stabilization. ECT has not been associated with fetal growth effects or toxicity.[24] Any discussion about ECT would require obstetrical (ob) involvement to examine for pre-existing obstetrical risk factors that may complicate the treatment.[25]

This form of treatment is a viable alternative for women with severe illness who do not want exposure to medications throughout their pregnancy and those who fail to respond to usual antidepressant treatments.

36. Is Repetitive Transcranial Magnetic Stimulation (rTMS) recommended during pregnancy?

This non-invasive treatment is relatively new, but it has been FDA approved for treatment-resistant depression. However, studies still need to be conducted in order to determine its safety for pregnant women. Repetitive transcranial magnetic stimulation (rTMS) treatment stimulates the cortical brain cells through the use of an electromagnet placed on the scalp. The magnet allows for synchronized electrical pulses to stimulate underlying brain tissues for mood stabilization.[26]

A case report of one pregnant patient who had both depression and anxiety noted improved mood with repetitive transcranial magnetic stimulation (rTMS).[27]

37. Which antidepressant medications are considered mild ones?

All antidepressants have pages of potential side effects listed in the *Physicians' Desk Reference* (PDR). The manufacturers of antidepressants are very clear on their product labeling, and they do not recommend the use of antidepressants in pregnant females. It is disclosed in the product information or package insert that there are no well-controlled studies of their medication for pregnancy, labor, or delivery. The pharmaceutical companies all advise that benefits and alternative treatments during pregnancy should be reviewed and documented prior to the health prescriber's recommendation of medication.

38. Does the placenta form a protective barrier from medications around the fetus?

No, all chemicals or drugs can cross the placenta and potentially impact the fetus.

39. Does the medical profession have guidelines for medication usage?

The Federal Drug Administration (FDA) designated the placement of a pregnancy label on medical information in response to legislation in 1979. The goal was to assist physicians in prescribing medications to pregnant females with regard to congenital abnormalities. Now the FDA is in the process of revamping this labeling system, because it really is not clinically useful. Most physicians usually abide by the standard of care in their community. In other words, they use the prescribing practices of other doctors in their specialty when they consider FDA guidelines.[28]

40. What are the category designations of the FDA?

The FDA lists the following information on its website for the various medication categorizations.

"Category A. Adequate, well-controlled studies in pregnant women have not shown an increased risk of fetal abnormalities.

"Category B. Animal studies have revealed no evidence of harm to the fetus; however, there are no adequate and well-controlled studies in pregnant women, or animal studies have shown an adverse effect but adequate and well-controlled studies in pregnant women have failed to demonstrate risk to the fetus.

"Category C. Animal studies have shown an adverse effect and there are no adequate and well-controlled studies in pregnant women, or no animal studies have been conducted and there are no adequate and well-controlled studies.

"Category D. Studies, adequate well-controlled or observational, in pregnant women have demonstrated a risk to the fetus. However, the benefit of therapy may out weigh the risk.

"Category X. Studies, adequate well-controlled or observational in animals or pregnant women have demonstrated positive evidence of fetal abnormalities. The use of this product is contraindicated in women who are or may become pregnant."[29]

41. Why don't physicians follow these category labels?

While these category designations seem simple and easy to understand, the FDA never intended that the labels would dictate treatment. Most pregnancies are not planned. The system does not address the impact of limited exposure to the fetus of an unplanned pregnancy where medication is discontinued at discovery of pregnancy. The research data reviewed to decide upon the initial FDA category was mostly obtained from animal data, not human. Once a category had been designated, updates with current information are rare. The letter designation does not provide enough useful information to assist in the risk versus benefit discussion between patients and their physicians.[30]

42. Can you give me an example of how the FDA label designations are not helpful?

An example would be the antidepressant Bupropion (Wellbutrin) that has the designation of a Category B. The Bupropion research data that met the criteria for placement in that category was based on animal data, not human studies. Reproductive studies conducted with rats and rabbits with doses seven – eleven times the average Bupropion human dosage did not indicate any harm to the animal fetus. In rabbits, a slightly increased risk of fetal abnormalities was found, but no increase in any specific abnormality. Despite the category B listing, Bupropion is prescribed in the psychiatric community with caution during pregnancy. Animal studies are not always predictive of human response.

Meanwhile, the most frequently prescribed antidepressants, the ssri are in category C. The ssri's safety data was obtained from the substantial prescriptions written by providers over the years. Fetal risk can potentially occur with both medications, but Bupropion has rat and rabbit data to support its safety for category B designation.[31]

43. **Are there other medications that carry an FDA category C rating that are similar to antidepressant medication?**

Most medications, including most antidepressants, are considered category C. To follow is a list from Briggs, Freeman, and Yaffe's book, *Drugs in Pregnancy and Lactation*, of other category C drugs.

Antibiotics (Anti-Infectives)
- Neomycin
- Bacitracin
- Chloramphenicol
- Griseofulvin
- Amantadine

Cholesterol-Lowering Agents
- Cholestyramine
- Fenofibrate
- Gemfibrozil

Artificial Sweeteners
- Aspartame (Category B/C)
- Saccharin

- Cyclamate

Cardiovascular Drugs
- Verapamil
- Phentolamine
- Digoxin
- Nifedipine
- Quinidine
- Procainamide
- Dilitazem
- Felodipine

Anti-Seizure Drugs
- Gabapentin
- Lamotrigine
- Oxcarbazepine
- Felbamate

Anti-Diabetic Drugs
- Chlorpropamide
- Glimepiride
- Glipizide
- Glyburide
- Tolazamide

Anti-Migraine Drugs
- Naratriptan
- Rizatriptan
- Sumatriptan

Herbs
- Echinacea
- Garlic
- Ginger
- Ginkgo Biloba
- Nutmeg
- Passion Flower
- St. John's Wort

Respiratory Drugs
- Dextromethorphan
- Hydrocodone
- Theophylline
- Aminophylline
- Beclomethasone Inhalers
- Triamcinolone Inhalers[32]

44. Should I be concerned about the medications my baby would be exposed to if I became pregnant today?

Everyone should readily identify prescription medications as chemicals of concern with the possibility of pregnancy. One should also include herbal agents, over the counter medication, and nutritional supplements. In addition, second-hand smoke, cigarettes, alcohol, and any illicit substances (marijuana and so on) have to be identified as a source of potential chemical exposure to your fetus. Some individuals would have to consider occupational and environmental exposure as well when they review their chemical risk.

45. **How do antidepressant medications function in the brain?**

In a very simple explanation, the brain of individuals with depressive illness is not able to produce or recognize enough happy hormones to maintain emotional wellness. Medications provide a replacement amount of happy hormones to the brain from a pool of three distinct families. In other words, antidepressant medication provides replacement therapy selected from the family of serotonin, dopamine, or norepinephrine. This concept of replacement is very similar to someone who has diabetes that requires insulin supplements.

46. **What medications are considered antidepressant medications?**

Serotonin Selective Reuptake Inhibitors (SSRI)

Brand Name (Generic Name)
- Prozac (fluoxetine)
- Zoloft (sertraline)
- Paxil (paroxetine)
- Luvox (fluvoxamine)
- Celexa (citalopram)
- Lexapro (escitalopram oxalate)

Tricylic Antidepressants (TCA)

Brand Name (Generic Name)
- Norpramin (desipramine)
- Sinequan, Adapin (doxepin)
- Tofranil (imipramine)

- Pamelor (nortriptyline)
- Surmontil (trimipramine)
- Vivactil (protriptyline)
- Anafranil (clomipramine)
- Elavil (amitriptyline)

Monamine Oxidase Inhibitors (MAOI)
Brand Name (Generic Name)
- Nardil (phenelzine)
- Parnate (tranylcypromine)
- Marplan (isocarboxazid)

Serotonin Norepinephrine Inhibitors (SNRI)
Brand Name (Generic Name)
- Effexor Tablets (venlafaxine)
- Effexor XR (venlafaxine)
- Remeron (mirtazapine)
- Remeron Sol Tabs (mirtazapine)
- Cymbalta (duloxetine)

Other Antidepressants
Brand Name (Generic Name)
- Serzone (nefazodone)
- Wellbutrin Tablets (bupropion)
- Wellbutrin SR (bupropion)
- Wellbutrin XL (bupropion)
- Desyrel (trazodone)
- Asendin (amoxapine)

47. **Are antidepressant medications safe during pregnancy?**

It depends upon your definition of safe. If safe for you means no potential problems, then all medications are risky. The serotonin family of antidepressants does not appear to increase the risk of congenital problems when the incidence is compared to pregnant women not on medications.

In the medical community, if medications are a choice in treatment, it has become the standard of care to consider first the serotonin family of antide-pressants. The long-term effects of antidepressant use during pregnancy remain unknown. There is always the possibility that these antidepressants might be associ-ated in the future with other potential side effects cur-rently not identified.

48. **What medications are considered in the serotonin family?**

The majority of patients today receive antidepressant medication from the serotonin family. Direct to con-sumer advertisements and the press have made the serotonin family such as Prozac, Paxil, Zoloft, Celexa, Luvox, and Lexapo quite popular. As a family class, serotonin drugs tend to promote calmness, reduce anxiety, reduce worry, and treat depression.

49. **Are there any differences among the safety data ob-tained for the Serotonin Selective Reuptake Inhibitor (SSRI) antidepressants?**

Since Prozac was the first SSRI inhibitor antidepressant

discovered, it has both the most research studies conducted and the largest sample population exposed. Paxil, Zoloft, Lexapro, and Celexa were all discovered later and have less research data when compared to Prozac. Celexa's safety data has been obtained from European research data as opposed to American studies.[33] The most recent SSRI manufactured, Lexapro, has limited research data about usage during pregnancy.[34] Lexapro's chemical structure is a mirror image of the well-known Celexa's chemical molecule. Many clinicians assume Lexapro safety data can be indirectly obtained from the Celexa pregnancy safety data.

50. Have there been observations of brain damage in children exposed to antidepressants?

Nulman, et al, reviewed the data of mothers in the Canadian Motherisk Teratology Information Study, which was published in 1997, whose babies had been exposed to tricylic antidepressants and/or to fluoxetine (Prozac) during pregnancy. Results of the study suggested that there was no significant impact of the antidepressants upon children exposed. The global IQ and language development was assessed between sixteen and eighty-six months in eighty children exposed to tricylic antidepressants, fifty-five children exposed to fluoxetine (Prozac), and eighty-four not exposed to any known chemical that might produce congenital defects.[35]

Nulman, et al, published another study in 2002 that followed and observed the pregnancy of mother-child pairs with forty-six exposed to tricylic antidepressants, forty exposed to fluoxetine, and thirty-six not exposed to medications. The children were, as in the prior study, tested for language development, global IQ, and temperament. Again the findings were similar with no adverse outcomes noted in ages fifteen to seventy-one months. It was observed that children of untreated depressed mothers had lower global IQ and less language development than those children exposed to antidepressant medication.[36]

Both these studies are limited by their small sample size, but they both concluded there is no significant difference in language, global IQ, or behavioral development in preschool and early school children exposed to medications during pregnancy.

51. What happens if my depression does not respond to the serotonin family of medications?

Despite SSRI's being the most popular antidepressants, not all patients respond to those agents. Less popular but effective antidepressants belong to the tricylics such as nortriptyline and desipramine. These tricylic medications are often used because of their long-standing history, but they have the risk of lowering blood pressure. In the 1970s, case reports suggested an association between tricylic first trimester pregnancy exposure and limb malformation. Later studies have not been able to support these earlier reports of increased congenital malformations.

If the patient has had numerous trials with medications and has finally responded to a medication with limited safety data for pregnancy, it might be decided after discussion with her health provider to stay on the medication. Effexor and Wellbutrin are not considered first-line agents for pregnancy but have been used to stabilize pregnant females.[37] There are no hard-core rules and guidelines. Ultimately, a medical decision is based upon the current medical information and the patient's mood stabilization in a risk versus benefit discussion. The intent of causing no harm to the mother and the unborn child influences the ultimate treatment recommendation.[38]

52. Are medication-exposed babies prone to low birth weight and/or increased medical complications?

Maternal depression during pregnancy can reduce appetite, which is often associated with low birth weight. The determination of antidepressant medication's impact upon infant weight cannot be fully assessed if the mother was depressed with an appetite reduction. Not all research studies about antidepressant medications during pregnancy fully consider the impact of maternal factors such as appetite loss during pregnancy, which can negatively affect the baby.

Historically, research studies did not always assess other maternal depressive behaviors such as the common use of alcohol, illicit drugs, nicotine, and exposure to second-hand smoke, which are factors known for a negative impact with pregnancy. This exclusion limits the reliability of some research findings that suggest po-

tential adverse outcome being associated with antide-
pressants-exposed babies.

Nonetheless, there are a few research studies that
clearly suggest infants exposed to SSRI antidepressant
medication have increased use of special care nurs-
eries and a tendency for premature births. These research
findings need to be replicated and further reassessed in
large population, placebo-controlled research studies for
definitive outcomes.[39]

53. Why did the FDA require a product labeling change for SSRI and SNRI antidepressant medications to include neonatal withdrawal syndrome and toxicity in newborns exposed during the third trimester?

Antidepressant use during pregnancy is never without
risk. The FDA issued a reminder after their review of the
available research data that third trimester exposure can
pose a risk to the baby. Adverse events observed in some
studies have been "respiratory distress, cyanosis, apnea,
feeding difficulties, vomiting, hypoglycemia, tremors,
jitteriness, and constant crying."[40] The required labeling will state that these symptoms are "consistent with
SSRI/SNRI discontinuation symptoms or direct toxic effects
of the drugs." Generally these symptoms are transient
and resolved within days or weeks.[41]

Medications should be administered only after a risk
versus benefit determination. The underlying cause of
the third-trimester fetal difficulty remains unknown. Al-
legations that the observed adverse outcomes stem directly from antidepressant fetal serotonin toxicity or

antidepressant withdrawal reactions still need further clarification.[42] This recent information highlights that antidepressant medication should only be administered during the third trimester of pregnancy after a risk versus benefit determination has been completed.

54. Does this warning suggest that medications should be discontinued in the third trimester because depressive illness is cured?

Pregnancy does not cure illness. The warning is a reminder to the health provider and the patient that medication use during pregnancy is not without risk. It suggests that the severity of illness should be demonstrated to warrant the risk of exposure to the baby. If you have self-destructive tendencies, lose touch with reality, and cannot function when depressed, your discontinuation of medications in the third trimester of pregnancy will not prevent relapse.

The recent FDA advisory suggests that infant exposure in the third trimester may be associated with risk of preterm delivery and potential risk of antidepressant withdrawal. Yet to discontinue antidepressant medications two weeks prior to your due date in order to prevent potential withdrawal for your baby may instead only increase your risk of illness relapse.

I have counseled many patients about the risks of these medications prior to this new FDA warning. Some have questioned my opinion since they have been informed of the drug's safety by expert books, the Internet, and many of their friends who had used these medications during pregnancy. The FDA warning is a reminder that the use of these medications is not without risk.

55. **I've heard that Monoamine Oxidase Inhibitors (MAOI) require dietary restrictions. Does that mean those medications are safer?**

Monoamines Oxidase Inhibitors (MAOI) are a type of antidepressants that require compliance with a restrictive diet. The drug interactions of MAOI's with the tyramine content of various foods, medicine, and beverages can trigger a hypertensive crisis — an abrupt sharp elevation in blood pressure that can cause a stroke.

There is limited information regarding safety of monoamine oxidase inhibitors in pregnancy. It is not usually recommended to use those medications during pregnancy. For a group of select pregnant females, MAOI are prescribed because the benefits clearly outweigh the potential risks.[43]

56. **Will antidepressant treatment during pregnancy prevent postpartum depression?**

No, taking antidepressant medication during pregnancy will not prevent postpartum depression.

57. **My antidepressant recently went from brand name to generic. How safe is the generic medication when compared to the brand name?**

The FDA considers generic products given an A rating to be therapeutically equivalent to the brand name. The assumption is made that products, which are therapeutically equivalent, have the same clinical effectiveness.[44] In my clinical practice, I have experienced that some patients relapse when forced to switch because of insurance requirements, while other patients have no problems when switched to generics. Patients who can afford it opt to pay the price for their brand name medication if their generic version did not provide the same symptom relief. The million-dollar question becomes who will relapse with a medication switch? Is the relapse rate due to a placebo effect or generic ineffectiveness? There is no clear answer.

The pregnancy research data has been obtained from brand name products. Generic pharmaceuticals have no requirements to demonstrate research data of their product safety or equivalence during pregnancy. The FDA assumes that generic products are therapeutically equal to brand name products when an A rating has been given.

The FDA publishes the *Approved Drug Product with Therapeutic Equivalence Evaluation* (the Orange Book), which identifies the therapeutic drug equivalence. An online version can be obtained monthly at http://www.fda.gov/cder/ob/default.htm.

58. I consider herbs safer than antidepressant medications for use during pregnancy. Where can I find more information about the product safety of herbs?

Before drugs are approved, the FDA requires pharmaceutical companies to demonstrate that their drugs do not cause cancer, damage organs, interfere with reproduction, and provide more benefit than harm. Nutritional supplements like St. John's Wort have no such requirements to provide safety data when the product is advertised to the public. Some herbal supplements state they have studies to support their usage. These studies are often limited in nature. They have not been required to adhere to the same strict standards as pharmaceutical companies to demonstrate product safety. Most information available on the Internet about dietary supplements is created to sell products.

The National Center for Complementary and Alternative Medicine (NCCAM), Clearinghouse's mission is to be the point of contact for scientifically based information on complementary and alternative medicine (CAM). It does not provide medical advice or make referrals to health providers. See the Resource appendix for contact information.

The National Center for Complementary and Alternative Medicine (NCCAM) and the National Library of Medicine (NLM) partnered to create CAM on PubMed. This web resource provides access to citations, full-text articles, and resources from large databases for free. Visit: http://www.nlm.nih.gov/nccam/camonpubmed.html.

General information about dietary supplements and how they may be regulated can be found at National Institute of Health Office of Dietary Supplements. Visit: http://ods.od.nih.gov/factsheets/DietarySupplements.asp.

General information about botanicals and a background on how they may be monitored can be found at the following site. Visit: http://ods.od.nih.gov/fact-sheets/botanicalbackground.asp.

Professionals in the medical community often access www.consumerlabs.com, which provides independent test results about health, wellness, and nutrition products. Products that have passed its test can bear the Consumer Labs seal of approval.

59. How is safety data determined for antidepressant medications?

The use of technology allows pregnant women exposed to antidepressant medication to be readily followed and their outcomes analyzed. Eli Lilly pharmaceuticals, the manufacturers of Prozac, were the first to establish a pregnancy register for their antidepressant medication users. All providers were encouraged to report the clinical information of their pregnant patients exposed to Prozac. Subsequently, most pharmaceutical companies now have a pregnancy registry to monitor outcomes of pregnant patients who use their medication.

Other sources of information collection include insurance companies with huge databases of their insured pregnant patients and academic medical centers that participate in clinical research.

Despite the studies on medication exposure, the sort of meaningful research required to determine safety in pregnant women is limited. Fear of lawsuits has made many pharmaceutical companies reluctant to expose themselves legally by supporting research to test medications on pregnant women. Existing databases for antidepressant usage during pregnancy include women who are predisposed to infertility, prior miscarriages, and other high-risk factors that may falsely increase adverse outcome results.

60. Are women with depressive illness more likely to require a cesarean section for delivery?

The limited data available would suggest that there is no association with depressive illness and mode of delivery.[45]

Chapter 7

Getting the Emotional Support I Need

In planning your pregnancy, it might be useful to create a supportive network of family and friends.

61. **How can I share my mental illness with others and not have them think I am crazy?**

Be Selective

Before you choose a person to share with, you will want to identify certain characteristics. Someone who accepts you unconditionally is a good candidate. Choose a person who always encourages you to achieve goals to the best of your ability. In addition, choose an individual who is sensitive to mental health issues and willing to understand your mental illness, even if they have had no personal encounters.

Timing and Setting

Identify the best time to share your concerns and take into consideration the most appropriate time and setting for a sensitive conversation. If your spouse loves football, it would probably not be a good idea to address your issues during a football game. Some individuals zone out completely after work; serious conversation should only occur after they have had some relaxation time. If you want someone to pay attention to your needs, be sensitive about the best time for them to receive communication.

Be Specific

Sometimes people have difficulty distinguishing sadness from depressive illness. You might consider sharing your symptoms as explained by your health professional.

Universal symptoms such as being forgetful, not sleeping, not concentrating, not retaining information, or loss of appetite can be readily understood. Be specific about how they can help you as well. You can delegate specific tasks like meal preparation, bill paying, grocery shopping, getting the mail, and even doing laundry. A supportive network can assist you with many of these everyday tasks.

Know What to Avoid

Often family and friends think that there is an event, person, or situation that triggered your illness. This makes them feel the need to help you resolve the stressful event to cure your depression. But, stressful situations or conversations can trigger a relapse of illness in a person already symptomatic. It is probably best for a person struggling with depression to avoid conflict and anxiety-prone conversations all together. I tell my patients to blame me for their inability to discuss certain topics and say something like, "My doctor told me that this topic is not to be discussed with anyone except her until I am well."

62. Could you give me an example of what I could say to a friend to encourage emotional support?

Here is a sample script for talking to someone about getting the emotional support you need. Let's say that Mary has a recent diagnosis of depression. She feels that a possible pregnancy next year will require her to establish a support system. During a lunch date, she will share her diagnosis with a supportive work colleague.

I went to see my doctor last winter for a routine physical exam because of my trouble with mood swings and feeling fatigued. My physical examination and blood work all came back normal. She referred me to a psychiatrist since it appeared to be depression. The psychiatrist agreed with the finding and prescribed a trial of antidepressant medications. The diagnosis was confusing to me, since I do not consider myself a depressed person. The doctor's explanation of my diagnosis did explain my behavior and difficulties though.

I really want to get pregnant this fall, but now I am worried about a possible relapse when I stop taking the medication. It is important for me to know that if I become pregnant there will be support. My goal is to remain stable for a few more months and then try to get pregnant. My depressive symptoms really scared me, and the active illness made my daily living so difficult. You have been so supportive of me, and I would like to share some concerns.

When I'm depressed I become stressed about completing simple tasks at work. I cannot sleep at night. I lose my appetite, and my concentration is so impaired that completing daily tasks is difficult. I get so tired and fatigued. For no particular reason, I can find myself crying. It is bad when I start to cry watching commercials on television or listening to songs on the radio.

My husband has agreed to pay the bills when my symptoms are active. I usually manage our budget, but that task seems so impossible when the illness is active. It can be difficult for me to make simple decisions of what to even buy for groceries and cook. My husband is now planning to cook or use take out from restaurants during the nine months of pregnancy. I am planning to explore catering services that deliver meals prepackaged weekly. You are such a great cook. It would be great if you would continue to invite us over for dinner.

I'm really concerned about poor concentration and focus with my active depressive symptoms. If you see me at work looking distracted, please let me know. We've

been walking during lunchtime. Please encourage me
to keep it up. When my depressive symptoms are active,
it makes me feel so tired even without being pregnant.
Exercise usually helps improve my moods and gives me
more energy.

Please remember that my inability to be my usual
self with you is not about our relationship but my de-
pressive illness behavior. Overall, I am very excited
about the thought of having a family. My doctors
have all reassured me that depression in remission is not
a contraindication for pregnancy.

63. What sort of role does my partner play in this pregnancy journey?

Your partner can be your major source of emotional support. Oftentimes your partner can provide a reality check for your irrational mood swings and sensitivities. Early in the pregnancy journey, your partner should be aware that your mood swings are related to the reproductive hormones and not to take it personally. Irritability, a common emotion during pregnancy, requires interpersonal interactions to be expressed. One is never irritable to oneself. These mood swings, which can be a normal event during pregnancy, can be extreme if magnified by underlying active depressive illness.

As a woman's body is changing during pregnancy, it is important to acknowledge its beauty. Many women consider being "fat" a negative experience. I have met some women who diet during their pregnancy to prevent weight gain. Some women don't want to gain weight during pregnancy because it affects their self-esteem and self-worth. Weight gain, body image, and self-esteem define self-worth for some women regardless of their pregnancy status. Your partner can challenge these negative mental images with unprompted statements of approval and affection, special little token gifts, cards, and flowers. Even a back massage can have a positive impact on the self-esteem of a pregnant lady.

During pregnancy, your partner needs to be easily located. If you are going out of town, identify someone who can be readily available if necessary. A pregnancy can easily justify the expense of a cell phone or pager.

During the pregnancy, stressful issues in the relationship should be minimized. If certain topics stir up unresolved extreme negative emotions for both parties, it may be time to seek professional help. A new baby will not erase deep-seated emotional conflicts in a relationship. Conflicts can be magnified by the additional responsibilities of a child. If the relationship has major conflicts in areas such as communication, trust, and finances, seek help. Furthermore, extreme responses to stressful events will only be magnified by active depressive symptoms.

Overall, it is most important for your partner to be emotionally available to you.

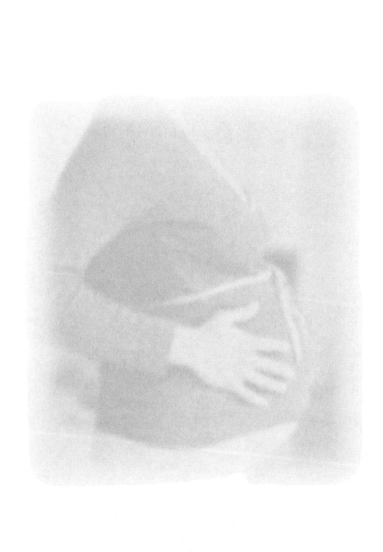

Chapter 8

What Should I Do Now?

In the mental health community, treatment recommendation is individually tailored to meet the needs of each pregnant female. This chapter will provide you with a framework to identify choices that feel comfortable to you. If you feel comfortable with your decision, you will easily comply with the treatment selected. Being honest with yourself and about your illness allows you to actively participate with your mental health provider about your options and increase compliance. To live worry-free with your treatment decision, you have to believe this is the best option for you and your baby. Base your decision upon the information available at this time and then let it go. Worrying and second-guessing your decision will only increase your stress levels, which can trigger your emotional illness.

64. What about the 1% rule? Is that an acceptable risk?

Don't assume because the risk is one percent that it can't happen to you. Rare and infrequent happens to someone; otherwise, that side effect would never have been reported. If you accept a treatment recommendation under the assumption that it is completely safe and risk free, especially with medications, you are mistaken. Health decisions should be made only after a careful review of the risks of the proposed treatment versus the benefits. It is important to be honest with yourself and your potential baby about your risk tolerance. If there is a problem with the baby, can you accept it or will you need to place blame or guilt on someone else? The proposed treatment should be reviewed extensively, and you must consider an honest assessment of your risk tolerance. Your final decision should determine that the benefits of treatment outweigh any risks.

65. How important is the correct diagnosis?

The options for the best treatment are greatly influenced by a correct diagnosis. Your symptoms and severity of illness will determine your treatment options.

Ask yourself these questions. Do you require hospitalization, become psychotic, self-destructive, and/or dangerously impulsive? Or do you just feel blah, cranky, overwhelmed, and would rather be left alone? Can you function daily when the symptoms of your illness are active, or do you need to be symptom free? Can you delegate responsibilities to someone else if your symptoms are active? Can you get the support you need to help you function with active illness?

A mild episode of depression may allow you to be symptomatic but not inhibit your daily functioning. Meanwhile, a severe bout of illness inhibits both your self-care and ability to function. Severe illness might warrant hospitalization or the use of various medications while pregnant. The ability to bond with your baby and fulfill the responsibilities of parenting can be inhibited if your illness becomes severe.

If you can't function, you'll need to have resources and a good support network available so that you can delegate your responsibilities.

66. Should I plan my pregnancy in order to be symptom free at conception?

Unfortunately, most often the pregnancies for women with depressive illness are unplanned. Women who are symptomatic with their illness at the time of conception require more psychiatric intervention in their first trimester as opposed to someone whose depressive symptoms are under control. If a person is actively depressed, she may require more medication or a change in medication in her first trimester. This is when the fetus is much more vulnerable.

Planning your pregnancy requires you to acknowledge your life patterns and respect your depressive illness. If you are planning to stop medications, you should consider your environmental stressors. Do not plan to stop your medications when your life is the most stressful.

Identify the most stressful time of year for you. If year-end for your job is June and you are responsible for that information, you might not want to stop your medication at that time for pregnancy planning.

67. **Should I continue the treatment that offers the best relief for my illness or are there risks in doing that?**

Treatment response does not change with pregnancy. If a treatment outcome was good before pregnancy, it will remain good with pregnancy. A prior history of response is very important in treatment selection and should be evaluated in light of risks versus benefits.

68. **Is it possible that an alternative treatment will provide me with the same symptom relief?**

An alternative treatment may provide adequate relief from your depression. You might obtain partial relief of your symptoms with risk factors you can tolerate. You have to honestly assess your ability to function while not feeling your best.

Depression is a way of life for some individuals. They refuse or have not responded to conventional treatment options. Individuals with untreated mild to moderate depression can still get through their day by exerting tremendous emotional effort. Life can be very overwhelming with active depressive illness. After struggling through the day, usually there are no energy reserves left, but some people adjust to these limitations. Individuals can function marginally by limiting their responsibilities or delegating their duties to others. You need to ask yourself if it is feasible for you to delegate your responsibilities during pregnancy or if you can identify caregivers for your infant.

You also need to assess your requirements to function at your best. It may be possible for you to function somewhat symptomatically with a less risky alternative treatment option.

69. What if I still have questions about pregnancy and depressive illness?

In the world of technology, the Internet affords the opportunity to answer many medical questions. You could easily enter a topic on a search engine and immediately have access to information. The alternative could be a website where medical personnel answer questions from scripted responses about your concerns. The Internet can provide tons of information that still must be individualized by your health provider.

Your doctor has access to your record, which provides vital information about your response to treatment and family history with your personalized risk factors. Once reviewed by your provider, your medical history becomes alive with your physical presence. Allow time for a meaningful patient-doctor relationship to develop, and rely on your health provider as your best source of answers for questions.

70. **When should I schedule an appointment with my mental health care provider to discuss pregnancy options?**

The moment you decide to have a baby is the day you should schedule an appointment with your mental health provider. Time is going to be required with your provider in order to answer all of the questions that surfaced from reading this handbook. If you see your psychiatrist for a fifteen-minute appointment, it is not realistic to anticipate that all of your questions will be answered during that time. In this case, scheduling multiple appointments might be helpful if your insurance allows it. Otherwise, it might be of benefit to pay out of your pocket for a longer session so that all of your questions can be answered at once.

You also may not be able to see a therapist the moment you decide to address your emotional issues. If you plan to use your insurance benefits, some program require a referral from your primary care physician. This referral requirement might require a prior appointment with your primary care physician to document your need for mental health services. Sometimes getting an appointment with a mental health professional is not an easy process. First, you have to determine a therapist's ability to take on new patients, and there may be a waiting list for initial appointments. Once you have started therapy, the initial sessions are history gathering, which will generally not provide immediate relief from your depressive symptoms.

Time and planning with your mental health professional will be required to address all of your concerns of pregnancy appropriately. I suggest you make your appointment as soon as your pregnancy becomes an immediate viable option.

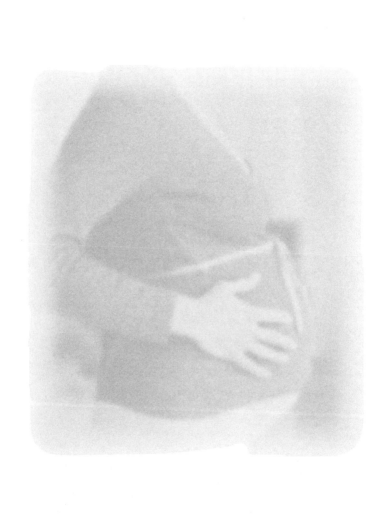

Afterword

It took the passage of time for me to fully appreciate the decision of teachers of clinical psychiatry to never dictate a particular treatment for all patients. Clearly, if the patient was self-destructive or psychotic the goal was universal, make sure the patient is safely and quickly stabilized. Otherwise, my teachers challenged me, explored my reasoning, and gave me clinical tools and scientific data to help me justify my proposed patient treatment plan. In the process of becoming a psychiatrist, I had to learn that patient treatment plans are individualized.

Likewise, my objectives for this book were to expand your knowledge, challenge your misconceptions, trigger a desire to further research the topic, and prompt a dialogue between the patient and their mental health provider to determine the best individualized treatment plan. The book was not written to endorse a particular treatment option during pregnancy. My years of clinical practice have only reinforced the belief that individualized treatment plans are required, as patient responses vary even with similar treatment.

Now that you have finished this handbook, I trust you have more tools to address this life-altering, "maybe baby" decision with your mental health provider. May you be at peace with your ultimate decision.

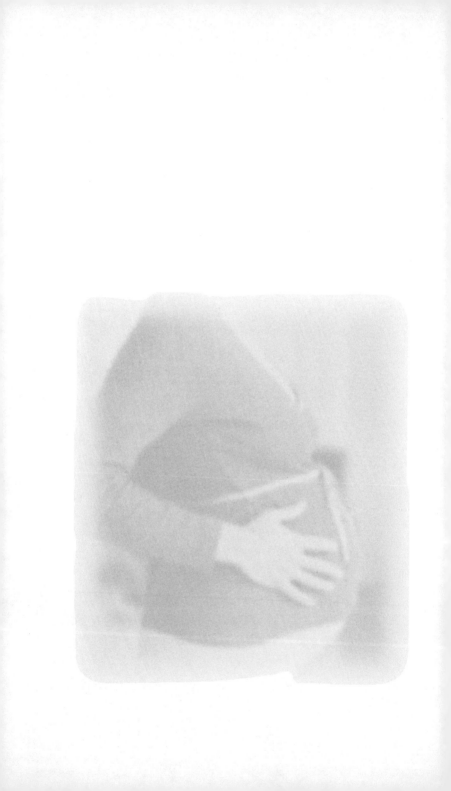

Additional Resources

American College of Obstetricians and Gynecologists (ACOG)
409 12th St. SW
PO Box 96920
Washington, DC 20090-6920
202-638-5577
www.acog.com

American College of Pediatrics (AAP)
14 Northwest Point Blvd.
Elk Grove Village, IL 60007
847-434-4000
www.aap.org

American Psychiatric Association
1000 Wilson Blvd., Suite 1825
Arlington, VA 22209-3901
888-357-7924 • 703-907-7300
www.psych.org

American Psychological Association
Office of Public Affairs
750 First St. NE
Washington, DC 20002-4242
800-374-2721 • 202-336-5500
www.apa.org

ConsumerLab.com, LLC
333 Mamaroneck Ave.
White Plains, NY 10605
914-722-9149
www.consumerlab.com

Depression after Delivery
91 E. Somerset St.
Raritan, NJ 08869
www.depressionafterdelivery.com

Depression and Bipolar Support Alliance
730 N. Franklin St., Suite 501
Chicago, IL 60610-7224
800-826-3632 • 312-642-0049
www.dbsalliance.org

Family Mental Health Foundation
1050 17th St. NW, Suite 600
Washington, DC 20036-5501
202-496-4977
www.fmhf.org

Federal Drug Administration (FDA)
Office of Women's Health
5600 Fishers Lane
Rockville, MD 20857-0001
www.fda.gov/womens
888-463-6332
The Orange Book Monthly Online Version
www.fda.gov/cder/ob/default.htm
FDA Pregnancy Registry
www.fda.gov/womens/registries/learnmore.html

Internal Revenue Service
Information on childcare tax credits
800-829-1040
www.irs.gov

Motherisk Program, The Hospital for Sick Children
555 University Ave.
Toronto, ON M5G 1X8
Canada
416-813-6780
www.motherisk.org

National Alliance for the Mentally Ill
Colonial Place Three
2107 Wilson Blvd., Suite 300
Arlington, VA 22201-3042
800-950-NAMI(6264) • 703-524-7600
www.nami.org

National Association of Social Workers
750 First St. NE, Suite 750
Washington, DC 20002-4241
800-742-4089
www.naswdc.org

**National Center for Complementary
and Alternative Medicine (NCCAM)**
PO Box 7923
Gaithersburg, MD 20898-7923
888-644-6226 • TTY 866-464-3615
Fax 866-464-3616 • Fax-on-Demand 888-644-6226
www.nccam.nih.gov
Search CAM on PubMed
www.nlm.nih.gov/nccam/camonpubmed.html

**National Institute of Health,
Office of Dietary Supplements**
6100 Executive Blvd.
Bethesda, MD 20892-7517
301-435-2920 • Fax 301-480-1845
http://dietary-supplements.info.nih.gov/

**National Institute of Mental Health,
Office of Communication**
6001 Executive Blvd., Room 8184, MSC 9663
Bethesda, MD 20892-9663
866-615-NIMH(6464) • 301-443-4513
www.nimh.nih.gov

National Mental Health Association
2001 N. Beauregard St., 12th Floor
Alexandria, VA 22311
800-969-NMHA(6642) • 703-684-7722
www.nmha.org

**Organization of Teratogenic
Information Service (OTIS)**
866-626-6847
www.otispregnancy.org

**U.S. Department of Labor,
Women's Bureau Clearing House**
Francis Perkins Building
200 Constitution Ave. NW
Washington, DC 20210
800- 827-5335
www.dol.gov/wb/

Endnotes

1. Glade B. Curtis and Judith Schuler, *Your Pregnancy Week by Week.* (New York: Da Capo Press, 2004), 29.
2. American Psychiatric Association, *Diagnostic and Statistical Manual of Mental Disorders.* (Washington, DC: American Psychiatric Press, 1994), 327.
3. Ibid, 325 – 326.
4. Ibid, 243 – 354.
5. Ibid, 377.
6. J. Raymond DePaulo, Jr., M.D., "Genetics of Bipolar Disorder: Where Do We Stand?" *The American Journal of Psychiatry* (American Psychiatric Association) 161, no. 4 (2004): 595 – 597.
7. Daniel N. Klein, Ph.D., Stewart A. Shankman, M.A., Peter M. Lewinsohn, Ph.D., Paul Rohde, Ph.D., and John R. Seeley, Ph.D., "Family Study of Chronic Depression in a Community Sample of Young Adults." *The American Journal of Psychiatry* (American Psychiatric Association) 161, no. 4 (2004): 646 – 653.
8. R. C. Kessler, K.A. McGonagle, M. Swartz, D.G. Blazer, and C.B. Nelson, "Sex and Depression in the National Comorbidity Survey I:

Lifetime Prevalence, Chronicity, and Recurrence." *Journal of Affective Disorders* (Elsevier Science Publishers) 29, no. 2–3 (1993): 85 – 96.

9. Andrea J. Rapkin, M.D., Judith Ann Mikacich, M.D., and Babak Moatakef-Imani, M.D., "Reproductive Mood Disorders." *Primary Psychiatry* (MBL Communications) 10, no. 12 (2003): 31 – 40.

10. R. Nonacs and L. S. Cohen, "Depression During Pregnancy: Diagnosis and Treatment Options." *Journal of Clinical Psychiatry* (Physicians Postgraduate Press) 63, suppl. 7 (2002): 24 – 30.

11. L. L. Altshuler, V. Hendrick, and L. S. Cohen, "Course of Mood and Anxiety Disorders During Pregnancy and the Postpartum." *Journal of Clinical Psychiatry* (Physicians Postgraduate Press) 59, suppl. 2 (1998): 29 – 33.

12. U.S. Equal Employment Opportunity Commission. *Pregnancy Discrimination Act of 1978.* http://www.eeoc.gov/abouteeoc/35th/the law/pregnancy_discrimination-1978.html.(accessed June 18, 2004).

13. U.S. Department of Labor. *Compliance Assistance — Family Leave and Medical Leave Act.* http://www.dol.gov/esa/whd/fmla/ (accessed November 10, 2003).

14. L. S. Cohen, L. L. Altshuler, Z. N. Stowe, et al. "Reintroduction of Antidepressant Therapy across Pregnancy in Women Who Previously Discontinued Treatment: A Preliminary Retrospective Study." *Psychother and Psychosom* (Canadian Psychiatric Association) 73, no. 4 (2004): 255 – 258.

15. I. S. Federenko and P. D. Wadhwa. "Women's Mental Health During Pregnancy Influences Fetal and Infant Development and Health Outcome." *CNS Spectrums.* (MBL Communications) 9, no. 3 (2004): 198 – 206.

16. U.S. Department of Health and Human Services. *Health, United States, 2004.* http://www.cdc.gov/nchs/data/hus/hus04trend.pdf#topic (accessed February 9, 2005).

17. Thomas Lathrop Stedman. *Stedman's Medical Dictionary, 26th edition.* (Baltimore: Lippincott, Williams, & Wilkins, 1995), 1461.

18. M. Spinalli. "Interpersonal Psychotherapy for Depressed Antepartum Women: A Pilot Study." *The American Journal of Psychiatry* (American Psychiatric Association) 154, no. 7 (1997): 1028 – 1030; M. Spinalli and J. Endicott. "Controlled Clinical Trial of Interpersonal Psychotherapy versus Parenting Education Program for Depressed Pregnant Women. ." *The American Journal of Psychiatry* (American Psychiatric Association) 160, no. 3 (2003): 555 – 562.

19. Lisa S. Segre, Ph.D., Scott Stuart, M.D., and Michael W. O'Hara, Ph.D. "Interpersonal Psychotherapy for Antenatal and Postpartum Depression." *Primary Psychiatry* (MBL Communications) 11, no. 3 (2004): 52 – 66.

20. A. Garland and J. Scott. "Cognitive Therapy for Depression in Women." *Psychiatric Annals.* (SLACK Incorporated) 32, no. 8 (2002): 465 – 476.

21. L. Altshuler, L. Cohen, et al. "The Expert Consensus Guideline Series: Treatment of Depression in Women, 2001." *Postgraduate Medicine.* (Mc Graw-Hill) 109 (2001): 45.

22. D. Oren, K. Wisner, et al. "An Open Trial of Morning Light Therapy for Treatment of Antepartum Depression." *The American Journal of Psychiatry* (American Psychiatric Association) 159, no. 4 (2002): 666 – 669.

23. K. A. Yonkers, K. L. Wisner, et al. "Management of Bipolar Disorder During Pregnancy and Postpartum Period." *The American Journal of Psychiatry* (American Psychiatric Association) 161, no. 4 (2004): 608 – 620.

24. L. Miller. "Use of Electroconvulsive Therapy During Pregnancy." *Hosp Comm. Psychiatry* (American Psychiatric Association) 45, no. 5 (1994): 444 – 449.

25. D. Polster and K. Wisner. "ECT — Induced Premature Labor, A Case Report." *Journal of Clinical Psychiatry* (Physicians Postgraduate Press) 60, no. 1 (1999): 53 – 54.

26. A. A. Gershon, P. N. Dannon, and L. Grunhaus. "Transcranial Magnetic Stimulation in the Treatment of Depression." *The American Journal of Psychiatry* (American Psychiatric Association) 160, no. 5 (2003): 835 – 845.

27. Z. Nahas, D. E. Bohning, et al. "Safety and Feasibility of Repetitive Transcranial Magnetic Stimulation in the Treatment of Anxious Depression in Pregnancy: A Case Report." *Journal of Clinical Psychiatry* (Physicians Postgraduate Press) 60, no. 1 (1999): 50 – 52.

28. S. Kweder "Labeling Products for Use in Pregnancy Moving Forward." (lecture, Psychopharmacology and Reproductive Transitions: Impact of Psychotropic Medications and Sex Hormones on Brain Functioning, Weight, and Reproductive Safety Symposium), American Psychiatric Annual Meeting, New York, NY, May 2, 2004.

29. U. S. Food and Drug Administration. *FDA Consumer Magazine* http://www.fda.gov/fdac/features/2001/301_preg.html (accessed September 26, 2004).

30. G. Koren, A. Pastuszak, and S. Ito. "Drugs in Pregnancy." *New England Journal of Medicine* (Massachusetts Medical Society) 338, no. 16 (1998): 1128 – 1136.

31. GlaxoSmith Kline to Stephanie Durruthy, **M.D.**, February 4, 2003, regarding the use of Wellbutrin in pregnant and lactating women.

32. Gerald G. Briggs, Roger K. Freeman, and Sumner J. Yaffe. *Drugs in Pregnancy and Lactation, 6th edition.* (Baltimore: Lippincott, Williams, & Wilkins, 2001), 1528 – 1538.

33. T. Heikkinen, U. Ekblad, P. Kero, et al. "Citalopram in Pregnancy and Lactation." *Clinical Pharmacology and Therapeutics* (Elsevier) 72, no. 2 (2002): 184 – 191.

34. PDR Staff. *Physician's Desk Reference, 59th edition* (Montvale, NJ: Thomson Healthcare, 2005), 1284.

35. I. Nulman, J. Rovet, D. Stewart, et al. "Neurodevelopment of Children Exposed in Utero to Antidepressant Drugs." *New England Journal of Medicine* (Massachusetts Medical Society) 336, no. 4 (1997): 258 – 262.

36. I. Nulman, J. Rovet, D. Stewart, et al. "Child Development Following Exposure to Tricylic Antidepressant or Fluoxetine Throughout Fetal Life: A Prospective, Controlled Study." *The American Journal of Psychiatry* (American Psychiatric Association) 159, no. 11 (2002): 1889 – 1895.

37. A. Einarson, B. Fatoye, et al. "Pregnancy Outcomes Following Gestational Exposure to Venlafaxine: A Multicenter Prospective Controlled Study." *The American Journal of Psychiatry* (American Psychiatric Association) 158, no. 10 (2001): 1728 – 1730; "Bupropion Pregnancy Registry, Interim Report." GlaxoSmith Kline (September 1, 1997 through February 29, 2004).

38. K. Wisner, D. Zarin, E. Holmboe, et al. "Risk-Benefit Decision Making for Treatment of Depression During Pregnancy." *The American Journal of Psychiatry* (American Psychiatric Association) 157, no. 12 (2000): 1933 – 1940.

39. L. Cohen, V. L. Heller, J. W. Bailey, et al. "Birth Outcomes Following Prenatal Exposure to Fluoxetine." *Biological Psychiatry* (Society of Biological Psychiatry) 48, no. 10 (2000): 996 – 1000; A. M. Costei, F. Kozer, et al. "Perinatal Outcome Following Third Trimester Exposure to Paroxetine." *Pediatrics & Adolescent Medicine* (American Medical Association) 156 (2002): 1129 – 1132; C. D. Chamber, K. A. Johnson, L. M. Dick, et al. "Birth Outcomes in Pregnant Women taking Fluoxetine." *New England Journal of Medicine* (Massachusetts Medical Society) 335, no. 14 (1996): 1010 – 1015.

40. E. Mechcatie, "FDA Panel Backs SSRI Label Change for Pregnancy," *Clinical Psychiatry News,* July, 2004.

41. U.S. Department of Health and Human Services. "Food and Drug Administration Center for Drug Evaluation and Research, meeting of the Pediatric Advisory Subcommittee of the Anti-Infective Drugs Advisory Committee (June 9, 2004)." http://www.fda.gov/ohrms/dockets/ac/04/transcripts/2004-4050T1.DOC (accessed October 9, 2004).

42. K. Laine, T. Heikkinen. "Effects of Exposure to Selective Serotonin Reuptake Inhibitors During Pregnancy on Serotonergic Symptoms in Newborns and Cord Blood Monoamine and Prolactin Concentrations." *General Psychiatry* (American Medical Association) 60, no. 1 (2003):

720 – 726; A. F. Schatzberg, P. Haddad. "Serotonin Reuptake Inhibitors Discontinuation Syndrome: A Hypothetical Definition." *Journal of Clinical Psychiatry* (Physicians Postgraduate Press) 58, suppl. 7 (1997): 5 – 10; H. Nordeng, R. Lindemann, et al. "Neonatal Withdrawal Syndrome after in Utero Exposure to Selective Serotonin Reuptake Inhibitors." *Acta Pædiatrica* (Taylor & Francis) 90 (2001): 288 – 291.

43. B. L. Gracious, K. L. Wisner. "Phenelzine Use throughout Pregnancy and the Puerperium: Case Report, Review of the Literature, and Management Recommendations." *Depression and Anxiety* (John Wiley) 6 (1997): 124 – 128.

44. Food and Drug Administration Center for Drug Evaluation and Research, Office of Pharmaceutical Science, *Orange Book, 23rd edition*, (Washington, DC: U.S. Department of Health and Human Services, 2003), xiii.

45. Wu J, Viguera A, et al. Mood disturbance in pregnancy and the mode of delivery. *American Journal of Obstetrics and Gynecology* (The National Medical Society) 187, no. 4 (2002): 864 – 867.

Bibliography

Altshuler, L. L., Cohen, L., Szuba, M. P., et al. "Pharmacologic Management of Psychiatric Illness During Pregnancy: Dilemmas and Guidelines." *The American Journal of Psychiatry* (American Psychiatric Association) 153, no. 5 (1996): 592 – 606.

Burke, K.C., Burke, Jr., J.D., Rae, D.S., and Regier, D.A., "Comparing Age of Onset of Major Depression and Other Psychiatric Disorders by Birth Cohorts in Five U.S. Community Populations." *General Psychiatry* (American Medical Association) 48, no. 9 (1991): 789 - 795.

Cohen, L. S., Nonacs, R., Viguera, A. C., et al. "Diagnosis and Treatment of Depression and Pregnancy." *CNS Spectrums* (MBL Communications) 9, no. 3 (2004): 209 – 216.

Cohen, L. S., Rosenbaum, J. F. "Psychotropic Drug Use During Pregnancy: Weighing the Risks." *Journal of Clinical Psychiatry* (Physicians Postgraduate Press) 59, suppl. 2 (1998): 18 – 28.

Corral, M., Kostaras, D. "Bright Light Therapy's Effect on Postpartum Depression." *The American Journal of Psychiatry* (American Psychiatric Association) 157, no. 2 (2000): 303 – 304.

Donis-Keller, H., Green, P., Helms, C., et al. "A Genetic Linkage Map of the Human Genome." *Cell* (Cell Press) 51, no. 2 (1987): 319 – 337.

Federenko, I.S., Wadhwa, P. D. "Women's Mental Health During Pregnancy Influences Fetal and Infant Development and Health Outcome." *CNS Spectrums* (MBL Communications) 9, no. 3 (2004): 198 – 206.

Fortier, I., Marcoux, S., Beaulac-Baillargeon, L. "Relation of Caffeine Intake during Pregnancy to Intrauterine Growth Retardation and Preterm Birth." *American Journal of Epidemiology* (Oxford University Press) 137, no. 9 (1993): 931 – 940.

Gabbard, Glen O. *Treatment of Psychiatric Disorders.* Washington DC: American Psychiatric Press, 1995.

Glover, V., Kammerer, M., "The Biology and Pathophysiology of Peripartum Psychiatric Disorders." *Primary Psychiatry* (MBL Communications) 11, no. 3 (2004): 37 – 41.

Halbreich, U. "Prevalence of Mood Symptoms and Depression During Pregnancy: Implications for Clinical Practice and Research." *CNS Spectrums* (MBL Communications) 9, no. 3 (2004): 177 – 184.

Harlow, B., Frigoletto, et al. "Determinants of Preterm Delivery in Low-Risk Pregnancies." *Journal of Clinical Epidemiology* (Elsevier Science Publishers) 49, no. 4 (1996): 441 – 448.

Hendrick, V., Stowe, V., Altshuler, L. L., et al. "Placental Passage of Antidepressant Medications." *The American Journal of Psychiatry* (American Psychiatric Association) 160, no. 5 (2003): 993 – 996.

Hollon, S. "Psychotherapy for Depressed Women." *TEN* (MedWorks Media) 4, no. 5 (2002): 54 – 59.

Hostetter, A., Ritchie, J. C., Stowe, Z. N. "Amniotic Fluid and Umblical Cord Blood Concentration of Antidepressants in Three Women." *Biological Psychiatry* (Society of Biological Psychiatry) 48, no. 10 (2000): 1032 – 1034.

Iqbal, M. M. "Effects of Antidepressant During Pregnancy and Lactation." *Annals of Clinical Psychiatry* (Taylor & Francis) 11, no. 4 (1999) 237 – 256.

Kessler, R. C., McGonagle, K. A., Swartz, et al. "Sex and Depression on the National Comorbidity Survey — Lifetime Prevalence, Chronicity, and Recurrence." *J Aff Disorder* (Elsevier Science Publishers) 29, no. 2–3 (1993): 85 – 96.

Kulin, N., Pastuszak, A., et al. "Pregnancy Outcome Following Maternal Use of the New Selective Reuptake Inhibitors." *JAMA* (American Medical Association) 279, no. 8 (1998): 609 – 610.

Kyrklund-Blomberg, N. B., Cnattingius, S. "Preterm Birth and Maternal Smoking: Risks Related to Gestational Age and Onset of Delivery." *American Journal of Obstetrics and Gynecology* (The National Medical Society) 179, no. 4 (1998): 1051 – 1055.

Leveno, K: *Williams Manual of Obstetrics.* New York: McGraw-Hill, 2003.

Linnet, K.M., Dalsgaard, S., Obel, C., et al. "Maternal Lifestyle Factor in Pregnancy Risk of Attention Deficit Hyperactivity Disorder and Associated Behavior: Review of the Current Evidence." *The American Journal of Psychiatry* (American Psychiatric Association) 160, no. 6 (2003): 1028 – 1040.

Llewllyn, A.M., Stowe, Z.A., Nemeroff, C. B. "Depression During Pregnancy and Puerperium." *Journal of Clinical Psychiatry* (Physicians Postgraduate Press) 58, suppl 15 (1997): 26 – 32.

Murkoff, H., Eisenberg, A., Hathaway, S. *What to Expect When You Are Expecting.* New York: Workman Publishing, 2002.

Newport, D. J., Stowe, Z. N., Nemeroff, C. B. "Parental Depression: Animal Models of an Adverse Life Event." *The American Journal of Psychiatry* (American Psychiatric Association) 159, no. 8 (2002): 1265 – 1283.

Nonacs, R., Cohen, L. S. "Depression During Pregnancy: Diagnosis and Treatment Options." *Journal of Clinical Psychiatry* (Physicians Postgraduate Press) 63, suppl. 7 (2002): 24 – 30.

Nulman, I., Koren, G. "The Safety of Fluoxetine During Pregnancy and Lactation." *Teratology* (Wiley-Liss, Inc.) 53 (1996): 304 – 308.

Orr, S. T., Miller, C. A. "Maternal Depressive Symptoms and the Risk of Poor Pregnancy Outcome: Review of the Literature and Preliminary Findings." *Epidemiologic Reviews* (Johns Hopkins University School of Hygiene and Public Health) 17, no. 1 (1995): 165 – 171.

Orr, S. T., James, S. A., Prince, C. B. "Maternal Prenatal Depressive Symptoms and Spontaneous Preterm Births among African-American Women in Baltimore, Maryland." *American Journal of Epidemiology* (Oxford University Press) 156, no. 9 (2002): 797 – 802.

Stead, L., Stead, M., and Kaufman, M. S. *First Aid for the Obstetrics and Gynecology Clerkship.* New York: McGraw-Hill, 2002.

Stewart, D. "Antidepressant Drugs during Pregnancy and Lactation. *International Clinical Pharmacology* (Lippincott, Williams, and Wilkins) 15, suppl. 3 (2000): S19 – S24.

Weinberg, M. K., Tronick, E. "The Impact of Maternal Psychiatric Illness on Infant Development." *Journal of Clinical Psychiatry* (Physicians Postgraduate Press) 59, suppl. 2(1998): 53 – 61.

Weissman, M., Warner, V., et al. "Offspring of Depressed Parents Ten Years Later. *General Psychiatry* (American Medical Association) 54, no. 10 (1997): 932 – 940.

Weissman, M., Gammon, D., et al. "Children of Depressed Parents. *General Psychiatry* (American Medical Association) 44, no. 10 (1987): 847 – 853.

Wisner, K., Perel, J., et al. "Tricylic Dose Requirement Across Pregnancy." *The American Journal of Psychiatry* (American Psychiatric Association) 150, no. 10 (1993): 1541 – 1542.

Index

backache, 9, 10
beclomethasone inhalers, 63
bereavement, 26
bipolar disorder, 28
birth weight, low, 49, 69
blood pressure, 6, 68, 72
body image, 83–84
books, self-help, 54
botanicals. *See* herbals
Braxton Hicks contractions, 9
breasts
    growth of, 8
    tenderness of, 7, 8
    tingling of, 7, 8
Bupropion, 60–61, 65

C

Celexa, 66, 67
cesarean section, 76
childhood memories, 17–19
chloasma, 9
chloramphenicol, 61
chlorproamide, 62
cholesterol-lowering
    drugs, 61
cholestyramine, 61
chronobiological treatment,
    55–56
cigarettes, 6, 48–49, 63, 69
citalopram, 65
cleanliness, 17–18
clomipramine, 65
COBRA, 42
cocaine, 26
cognitive behavioral therapy, 52
concentration, 82
congenital abnormalities, 58,
    66, 67, 68
consistency, 15–16, 16–17
constipation, 9, 10

contraceptives, 5
contractions, Braxton Hicks, 9
cramps, in legs, 10
crying, 8, 38, 70
cyanosis, 70
cyclamate, 61
Cymbalta, 65

D

death, 26
depression, 23–39
    diagnosis of, 25, 88–89
    and family history, 33–34
    and genetics, 33–34
    impact on fetus of, 48–49
    increased chance of, with
        pregnancy, 37
    mild, 29
    moderate, 29
    physical signs of, 38
    postpartum, 10, 12, 72
    risk factors for, 33–34,
        37–38
    severe, 29–30
    stigma of, 48
    symptoms of, 25–26
    treatment of (*See* treat-
        ment, of depression)
    types of, 26–28
    vs. sadness, 24–25
desipramine, 65
Desyrel, 65
dextromethorphan, 63
diabetes, medications for, 62
diet, 6, 48–49
    and artificial sweeteners,
        61–62
    and MAOI drugs, 72
dietary supplements. *See*
    herbals; *specific supplements*

digoxin, 62
dilitazem, 62
disability benefits, 41–42
dizziness, 9
doctors, hours of, 6
dopamine, 64
doxepin, 65
drugs, 57–76. *See also* herbals
  anti-seizure, 62
  antibiotic, 61
  antidepressant, 64–73
  cardiovascular, 62
  categorization of, and pregnancy, 58–59
  cholesterol lowering, 61
  determination of safety data for, 75–76
  diabetic, 62
  fetal exposure to, 63, 66, 70–71
  function of, in brain, 64
  generic *vs.* brand name, 72–73
  labeling of, 58
  for migraines, 62
  respiratory, 63
  and side effects, 57–58
  and unplanned pregnancy, 60
DSM IV (Diagnostic and Statistical Manual of Mental Disorders IV), 25
duloxetine, 65
dysthymia, 27

E

echinacea, 63
EEOC (Equal Employment Opportunity Commission), 45
Effexor, 65, 69

Elavil, 65
electroshock therapy (ECT), 56–57
emotional support. *See* support, emotional
epilepsy, medications for, 62
Equal Employment Opportunity Commission (EEOC), 45
escitalopram oxalate, 65
euphoria, 28
exercise, 83
eyes, swelling of, 10

F

false labor, 10
Family and Medical Leave Act of 1993 (FMLA), 43, 44
family history, and depression, 33–34, 37
fatigue, 7, 8, 13–14, 26
FDA (Federal Drug Administration), 58, 73
fear, 14–15
feet, swelling of, 9, 10
felbamate, 62
felodipine, 62
fenofibrate, 61
fighting, 18–19
finances, 38, 41–45, 82
  as trigger for depression, 26
first trimester. *See* trimester
fluoxetine, 65, 66–68
fluvoxamine, 65
FMLA (Family and Medical Leave Act of 1993), 43, 44
forgetfulness, 38
Freud, Sigmund, 24–25

G

gabapentin, 62

migraine, medications for, 62
mirtazapine, 65
miscarriage, 76
money, 38, 41–45, 82
  as trigger for depression, 26
monoamine oxidase in-
  hibitors, 65, 72
mood swings, 8, 28
murder, 49

N

naratriptan, 62
Nardil, 65
National Center for Complementary and Alternative
  Medicine (nccam) Clear-
  inghouse, 74
National Library of Medicine
  (nlm), 74
nausea, 7, 9
nccam. *See* National Center for
  Complementary and Alternative Medicine (nccam)
  Clearinghouse
nefazodone, 65
negativity, 14, 19
Neomycin, 61
nervousness, 14–15
neutrality, 14
nifedipine, 62
norepinephrine, 64
Norpramin, 64
nortriptyline, 65
numbness, of upper
  extremities, 10
nutmeg, 62

O

organization, 15–16
oxcarbazepine, 62

P

Pamelor, 65
parenting, 12–13
  and anxiety, 14–15
  and consistency, 16–17
  and memories of own
    childhood, 17–19
  and negativity, 14
  and organization, 15–16
  and patience, 15
  and socialization, 16
Parnate, 65
paroxetine, 65
partners, 83–84
passion flower, 63
patience, 15
Paxil, 66, 67
phenelzine, 65
phentolamine, 62
phototherapy, 55–56
physical abuse, 18
placenta, 48, 58
planning, of pregnancy, 89–90
play, 18
postpartum depression, 10,
  12, 72
pregnancy, initial signs of, 7
Pregnancy Discrimination Act
  (1978), 42, 45
premature birth, 69, 71
prenatal care, 6
procainamide, 62
protriptyline, 65
Prozac, 64, 66–68
psychodynamic therapy, 52
psychotherapy, 50–56
  cognitive behavioral, 52
  definition of, 50–51
  effectiveness of, 51–53
  finding provider of, 54–55
  frequency of, 53

About the Author

Stephanie Durruthy, M.D., is a board-certified psychiatrist in private practice. A former clinical director of the Johns Hopkins Bayview Psychiatric Day Hospital, Dr. Durruthy is currently a faculty member of the Johns Hopkins School of Medicine. She is a frequent lecturer on and an advocate for women's health issues.

After receiving her undergraduate degree from Cornell University in biological sciences, she earned her medical degree from Hahnemann Medical College in Philadelphia. Dr. Durruthy subsequently completed her psychiatric residency training at St. Vincent's Hospital and Medical Center in New York City. She completed a fellowship in Psychiatric Administration at the University of Maryland.

As a member of the American Psychiatric Association, she serves on the Committee of Women, a committee organized to promote women's health issues. She is a member of the Association of Women's Psychiatrist.

As a psychiatrist, mother, and woman, Dr. Durruthy is a strong voice on behalf of women and their mental health.

Ordering Information

Mindsupport books are available online and at your favorite bookstore.

Quantity discounts are available to qualifying institutions.

All Mindsupport, LLC books are available to the booktrade and educators through all major wholesalers.

For more information, email the publisher at
info@mindsupport.com
or visit
www.mindsupport.com